BARRON'S DOG BIBLES

Beagles

Eve Adamson

BARRON'S

Acknowledgments

So many people helped guide and educate me throughout the process of writing this book. Thanks to Sue Pearson, whose love for Beagles and skill at training them (and any dog) helped inform this text. Thanks to Dr. Charles Kitchell, for sharing his vast knowledge of Beagle history with me. Thanks to the many, many small hobby breeders and other Beagle people who have added to my Beagle knowledge over the many years that I have been writing. Thanks to my next-door-neighbor Beagle, for exposing me to the true and fantastic range of noises Beagles can make if they really put their minds to it. And finally, thanks to Caroline Coile. She knows why.

About the Author

Eve Adamson is an award-winning freelance pet writer and dedicated Beagle fan who has written or co-authored 12 books about companion animals. She is a contributing editor to *Dog Fancy* magazine, a columnist for *AKC Family Dog* magazine, a columnist for *Pet Product News International*, and a member of both the Dog Writers' Association of America and the Cat Writers' Association Inc. She lives in Iowa City with her family. Find out more about Eve on her website at *www.eveadamson.com*.

All information and advice contained in this book has been reviewed by a veterinarian.

A Word About Pronouns

Many dog lovers feel that the pronoun "it" is not appropriate when referring to a pet that can be such a wonderful part of our lives. For this reason, Beagles are described as "he" throughout this book unless the topic specifically relates to female dogs. This by no means infers any preference, nor should it be taken as an indication that either sex is particularly problematic.

Photo Credits

Tara Darling: viii, 8, 75, 81, 114, 133, 148, 154; Cheryl A. Ertelt: 110; Isabelle Farncail: 96; Jean M. Fogle: 11, 77, 79; Isabelle Francais: 20, 100, 127, 131; Paulette Johnson: 3, 9, 10, 13, 16, 18, 23, 25, 28, 29, 30, 35, 38, 41, 44, 46, 48, 50, 52, 54, 56, 57, 58, 60, 61, 63, 65, 66, 68, 70, 74, 76, 85, 86, 89, 90, 95, 98, 103, 104, 105, 107, 109, 116, 117, 118, 119, 120, 121, 122, 125, 129, 130, 134, 137, 139, 144, 147; Pets by Paulette: 72, 82, 99, 143; Shutterstock: i, iii.

Cover Credits

Front cover: Shutterstock; back cover: Tara Darling.

All inquiries should be addressed to:
Barron's Educational Series, Inc.
250 Wireless Boulevard
Hauppauge, New York 11788
www.barronseduc.com

ISBN-13 (book): 978-0-7641-6228-2
ISBN-10 (book): 0-7641-6228-4
ISBN-13 (DVD): 978-0-7641-8678-3
ISBN-10 (DVD): 0-7641-8678-7
ISBN-13 (package): 978-0-7641-9624-9
ISBN-10 (package): 0-7641-9624-3

Library of Congress Catalog Card No: 2008041326

Library of Congress Cataloging-in-Publication Data
Adamson, Eve.
    Beagles / by Eve Adamson.
        p. cm.— (Barron's dog bibles)
    Includes index.
    ISBN-13: 978-0-7641-6228-2 (book)
    ISBN-10: 0-7641-6228-4 (book)
    ISBN-13: 978-0-7641-8678-3 (DVD)
    ISBN-10: 0-7641-8678-7 (DVD)
    ISBN-13: 978-0-7641-9624-9
    ISBN-10: 0-7641-9624-3
    [etc.]
    1. Beagle (Dog breed) 2. Beagle (Dog breed)—
Pictorial works. I. Title.

SF429.B3A33 2009
636.753'7—dc22
                                        2008041326

Printed in China

9 8 7 6 5 4 3

CONTENTS

CONTENTS

PREFACE

The first Beagle I ever met was named Lucy. She lived in the house behind ours, and I babysat for the family, who also had a baby. I liked the baby, but I loved Lucy. I could relate to her. She was friendly and funny, an insatiable Chowhound, and she had a mind of her own. She didn't just sit there waiting for me to do something. She was a busy dog with an agenda, which sometimes involved couch meditation, but more often involved amusing herself in a variety of ways, from tracking down snacks to playing her own silly games with rules she invented—games she sometimes let me play, too. As a teenager, I could relate to that. The world was our playground, and we just wanted to have fun.

The more Beagles I met over the years, and the more I wrote about Beagles for magazines like *Dog Fancy*, the more I realized that Lucy was a classic, quintessential Beagle: Driven by her nose, her love of food, her natural wit, her intense curiosity, and an abiding affection for the human race.

Few breeds are as easy-going, kid-friendly, playful, affectionate, and cheerful as the Beagle, and Beagles are also a lot smarter than people tend to give them credit for. Snoopy writes novels on top of his dog house and entertains fantasies of battles in the sky with the Red Baron. I don't think that's such a stretch. Beagles have eyes that suggest the wheels are turning and life is bigger than it looks from the door of a dog house. Living with a Beagle—and trying to stay one step ahead—will quickly support that theory.

Mischievous? Witty? Natural comedians? Escape artists? Beagles are all those things and more. If you are lucky enough to have a Beagle as a member of your family, then I hope you will enjoy this book and find information inside that you can use to make your life together happier, more fun, and easier. If you are considering bringing a Beagle into your life, then may this book help guide your decision in the right direction. Beagles aren't for everybody. They need attention, care, and monitoring, they can't be trusted off leash, and they need protection from their scent-driven single-mindedness.

If you are one of those people who are meant to have a Beagle, then let this book be your guide. It is written with great respect for a breed I love, and with the sincere wish that you and your Beagle can live happily together in harmony and with mutual affection for a very long time.

Eve Adamson

Chapter One

All About Beagles

Picture the Beagle, with his merrily wagging tail, cheerful disposition, generous bark, and classic good looks. Picture him playing with the kids in the backyard, or baying after the scent trail of a rabbit in the woods, or resting his chin on your lap and looking up at you with his big brown eyes. Picture him tossing his favorite toy in the air, chasing a tennis ball, begging for a treat, snoozing on the couch, even winning the biggest dog show in the United States.

Winning the biggest dog show in the world? A Beagle? Yep, a Beagle named Uno did just that in 2008 when he took Best in Show at the famed Westminster Kennel Club dog show in New York City. Sorry, pampered Poodles, trimmed terriers, and spiffy sporting breeds. If a simple, wash-and-wear, happy-go-lucky Beagle can be a good old-fashioned best friend at home and Best in Show among the canine glitterati in New York City, can anything stop him?

A Beagle may sound like the ideal family dog, the perfect friend for kids, and a lovable companion to boot. Beagles do indeed have some uniquely wonderful qualities, but they also have a few specific traits and requirements that make them unsuitable for some people in some situations. While many prospective dog owners think they want a Beagle, the very qualities that make the breed unique can also be difficult to tolerate.

Life with a Beagle can be fantastic or frustrating. The key to assuring the former instead of the latter is to understand what makes a Beagle tick and what living with a Beagle really means. Beagles really can be as witty as Snoopy, as courageous as Underdog, as sweet as Shiloh, and as unassuming as Uno, but they also live by their noses and put good smells above anything else. Even people! They love kids, pal around with other dogs, and will give almost anybody the benefit of the doubt, but you can't train them never to bark and in some cases, the urge to dig is non-negotiable.

Beagles are portable, affectionate, easy-going, and, frankly, adorable, but some people get annoyed when the Beagle refuses to listen, or puts them second to a bag of treats. Beagles have a classic look: floppy ears, big brown eyes, and tri-colored coats (although they can come in many colors and patterns, as you'll soon find out), but they also shed all over the house. Versatile and athletic, Beagles can perform in competitions from field trials and tracking tests to agility and rally, but getting a Beagle to the level of a winner takes a lot of work.

BE PREPARED! Are You Ready for a Beagle?

Consider these questions before purchasing a Beagle:

1. Can you handle a dog that only listens to you when he isn't busy following a luscious scent trail, chasing a butterfly, or barking at the neighbors?
2. Will you be happy with a dog who will only work for food?
3. Can you manage a dog who can't be trusted off the leash or outside the fence...ever?
4. Are you rattled by excessive barking, baying, and even a little howling now and then? Are you prepared for some sounds you've never heard any other dog make before? What about the neighbors knocking on your door asking, "What's going on in there?"
5. Can you just say no to that cute pleading face when you know perfectly well your Beagle has had enough treats already? Can you exercise the willpower he doesn't have?

If you want a Beagle to do what he does best—play the role of loyal and faithful companion—you are on the right trail, but only by understanding why the Beagle exists in the first place can you begin to envision why this sometimes silly and sometimes stubborn scenthound acts the way he does and needs the things he needs.

In this chapter, you'll follow that trail back to its origins and take a look into the Beagle's history for clues. Then, you'll get a closer look at the official breed standard describing the ideal Beagle. By the end of this chapter, you'll be well on your way to understanding exactly what makes a Beagle a Beagle, and why your Beagle has those wonderful qualities you love . . . as well as those frustrating qualities that make you want to howl.

The Merry Little Hound

You might know dogs, but do you know hound dogs?

A Beagle is a much different animal than a Labrador Retriever, a Rottweiler, a Yorkshire Terrier, a Greyhound, or even his distant cousin, the Foxhound. While these are all dogs with four legs, tails, and the ability to bark, the sporting, working, and toy breeds, and the sighthounds and scenthounds, have all been specifically developed over centuries of selective breeding to do very different things. Even within a group of dogs—in this case, hounds—different breeds have different qualities.

One of the hound group's most prominent—and difficult—characteristics is independence. While sporting breeds like retrievers tend to look to people for direction, hounds don't. They have been bred to think for themselves and make their own decisions, so when you tell your Beagle what to do, he may not necessarily agree. He might even think that you (with your inferior sense of smell) don't have all the information you need to tell him what's what.

It's not that the Beagle has delusions of grandeur. Far from it. He's just acting the way he's been bred to act, and it's tough to argue with centuries of selective breeding. For people, the Beagle's independent spirit and highly developed nose have been very important qualities from the beginning. Those who created him wanted the Beagle to act that way, and Beagles are the way they are for some very good reasons.

Beagle Beginnings

Writing and art dating back to ancient Greece suggests that Beagle-like dogs were used for hunting. Some people believe Beagles are one of the oldest breeds in the history of dogs, and may have even been the very first scent hounds. Not everybody agrees, but because ancient Greek writings mention small dogs used for hunting hare, the theory is out there. Could these have been ancient Greek proto-Beagles?

Fun Facts

Legend has it that King Arthur kept a pack of small white hunting hounds bearing a remarkable resemblance to the modern Beagle. Beagles of the Round Table?

Throughout the Middle Ages, many Europeans hunted with dogs. When William the Conqueror came from Normandy to invade England in 1006, he brought hounds with him. Some of these were sight hounds (similar to Greyhounds), but many were white scent hounds, called Talbot Hounds. These dogs quickly became popular in England, and as always happens when any dog becomes fashionable, many people began to breed them. Eventually, two types of smaller hounds evolved: the Northern Hound and the Southern Hound. The Northern Hounds, or North Country Hounds, tended to be quicker, more agile, with longer, more pointy muzzles. The Southern Hounds were slower, with longer ears and lower voices.

British Beagles

Now firmly entrenched in England, hounds began to develop in new ways and hunters began to divide them into even more specific groups. By the middle of the eleventh century, the aristocracy had embraced sport hunting and were using packs of hunting hounds to flush out pheasants, hare, deer, and other animals—including the foxes that would later

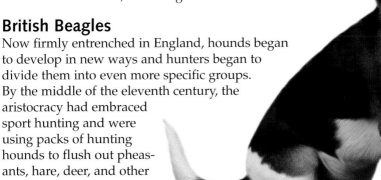

FYI: The Toy Dog Craze

Is a pocket, glove, toy, teacup, or Queen Elizabeth Beagle really a Beagle? Today, in an effort to profit from the toy dog craze, many breeders are purposefully breeding extra-small Beagles and advertising them by these and other catchy names. While there is historical precedent for these so-called varieties, the current breed standard does not recognize the pocket Beagle, or any other undersized version. While every breeder will occasionally get a very small puppy in a litter, these runts often have serious health problems, and many don't survive. Some suffer from dwarfism and have short legs. This is obviously not a sign of a healthy, correct Beagle. Smaller Beagles also tend to be more hyperactive, in general. If you decide to purchase a small Beagle, be wary. No ethical breeder will charge *more* money for these tiny guys. If anything, they should cost less because they don't fit the breed standard and aren't eligible for the show ring.

become such popular quarry. They often divided hound dogs into packs according to size. Larger hounds would chase larger, faster animals such as wolves and deer, while smaller hounds were used for smaller game such as rabbits and squirrels.

Smaller hounds also moved more slowly, making them well-suited to hunters on foot rather than on horseback. These smaller hounds were sometimes called "Begles." The name probably comes from an older word, *begueule*, which means "gape-throated" and may have had something to do with the baying sound the dogs made.

The Beagle as we know him didn't really exist in those days. Dogs were known by many different names, and there was no official standard to separate one breed from another; they were simply characterized by what the dogs could do and, to a lesser extent, by how they looked. Dividing dogs into breeds with specific names and qualities came much later, when dog shows became popular.

Still, these little hounds, or "Begles," continued to be popular. They also changed with the fashions. At times in history, these little hounds were bred to be extremely small, some just five inches tall. Queen Elizabeth I was a particular fan of these tiny "Pocket Beagles," which inspired breeders to make these early ancestors of the breed smaller and smaller. These little guys weren't very hardy for hunting. They often had to be carried on horseback to the hunting site, as not to wear themselves out before the actual hunt began. Written accounts note that these tiny dogs had excellent noses, but they weren't structurally sound. Many succumbed to distemper or were simply too slow to be useful.

During the nineteenth century, a particularly famous English Beagler named Reverend Phillip Honeywood, who lived in Essex, put a stop to the trend toward tiny Beagles. He wanted to breed a larger, sturdier dog that could run all day without tiring, but that would still be small enough to chase hare and rabbit, and follow on foot. His dogs became so popular that they sparked a renewed interest in "beagling" (hunting rabbits with Beagles) in England. Honeywood and his friends were sometimes called the "Merry Beaglers of the Meadows," and three of the group along with a large pack of Beagles were immortalized in a painting by Henrey Hall titled *The Merry Beaglers* (1845).

In 1873, the Kennel Club of England officially recognized the Beagle as a unique breed. A written Beagle breed standard was published in 1895 and the Kennel Club held its first Beagle dog show in 1897. The Beagle was finally, officially, a Beagle.

From England to America

Beagles have been chasing rabbits across the American continent for hundreds of years, even as they were evolving across the pond. Americans have been hunting rabbits with hound dog packs and braces (pairs) since the seventeenth century, but these early Beagle ancestors looked more like Dachshunds than the Beagles we know today.

Breed Truths

Beagles have changed in appearance over the centuries, but a few key characteristics have stayed the same. To be successful at hunting, Beagles must have:

- a keen sense of smell, to proficiently track quarry.
- a loud voice (tongue), so the hunter can hear what they are doing and where they are going.
- independence, because if something happens out in the field—an encounter with a predator, for example—the Beagle must make decisions without help from the hunter lagging behind.
- dog-friendliness, because Beagles usually work in packs or pairs and can't start fights with other dogs when they should be concentrating on the scent trail.

This changed during the 1870s, when General Richard Rowett of Carlinville, Illinois, imported a few British Beagles from England. General Rowett was a wealthy man who kept only the finest horses and livestock, so when he became interested in Beagles, he would settle for nothing less than dogs from the very finest British packs.

Rowett's dogs became so well-known and respected that they changed the face of the Beagle in America. Beagles became more uniform in size and appearance, and started to look like an actual breed, rather than a motley crew of random hound dogs. General Rowett bred Beagles that were both excellent pack dogs and good-looking enough to win in the show ring. Beagles became prettier, but they could still hunt rabbits with the best of the hounds. And that's when America really fell in love with the Beagle.

In 1888, the National Beagle Club formed in the United States, and competitive field trials became more and more popular. At this time, Beagles were divided into two sizes: 13 inches and under, or 13 to 15 inches. This division still stands today.

Rabbits are still hunted with Beagles, but today, Beagles do much more than hunt. Some compete in obedience trials, hunting tests, or tracking. Others are aces at the obstacle course sport called agility, or prefer a less intense form of competitive obedience known as rally. Many work as therapy dogs or service dogs. Some even work for the U.S. government, sniffing out illegal contraband at airports. But for most Beagles, the most important job is family companion, a post at which the breed truly excels.

Beagle Time Line

550 B.C.: The Laconian Hound, a dog resembling a Beagle, is pictured on a slab of marble from ancient Sparta. This piece of pre-Beagle art is on display at the Acropolis Museum in Athens, Greece.

400 B.C.: Xenophon wrote a book in which he referred to small hare-hunting hounds. He describes the Laconian Hound's conformation, which sounds a lot like a modern 13-inch Beagle.

200 A.D: Beagle-like hounds coursing hare and fox with men on horseback are depicted on a Roman North African mosaic.

1066: When William the Conqueror, aka the Duke of Normandy, was crowned King of England, he brought a French breed, the Talbot Hound, to England from France. This dog was later known as the Southern Hound.

1350: Count Gaston de Foix wrote of two separate types of hounds: larger hounds called Rachys and smaller hounds called Brachys. The larger hounds may have been ancestors of the Foxhound, while the smaller hounds were possibly ancestors of the Beagle.

1600: Queen Elizabeth I kept a hunting pack of "singing beagles," known for their merry and loud voices when they were following a scent trail.

1642: In Ipswich, Massachusetts, the first documented rabbit hunt using hound dogs occurred in the United States.

1650: Castiglioni, an Italian artist, visited England and painted portraits of many Beagle-like dogs.

1792: Printed in *Sporting Magazine*: "Of those dogs which are kept for the business of the chase in this country, the [B]eagle is the smallest, and is only used in hunting the hare. Though far inferior in point of speed to that animal, it follows by the exquisiteness of its scent, and traces her footsteps through all her various windings with great exactness and perseverance. Its tones are soft and musical, and add greatly to the pleasures of the chase."

1857: The famous writer Stonehenge, aka Dr. John Henry Walsh, wrote the first official Beagle breed standard. He based this standard on his study of Cockermouth Beagles in northwest England.

1859: Beagle packs were first included in the list of hound packs published in London sporting newspapers.

1870: General Richard Rowett, from Carlinville, Illinois, brought the first quality Beagles to the United States, and these were among the first Beagles entered in dog shows.

1873: The Kennel Club, England's national breed registry, officially recognized the Beagle breed.

1876: The first Beagles appeared in dog shows in the United States.

1884: In order to promote the Beagle as a breed in conformation dog shows, the American-English Beagle Club, also known as the American Beagle Club, formed.

1885: Blunder #3188 was the first Beagle registered with the American Kennel Club.

1890: The National Beagle Club held its first field trial in New Hampshire.

1891: Beagle and Harrier fanciers in England formed the Association of Masters of Harriers and Beagles, in order to distinguish Beagles from Harriers and record each in separate stud books. For the first time in England, interbreeding between Beagles and Harriers was discouraged.

1927: The Wisconsin Beagle Club held its first conformation show, and continues to hold conformation shows for Beagles, earning it the distinction as the oldest Beagle conformation competition in the United States.

1957: The current Beagle breed standard was officially approved by the American Kennel Club.

1970: The National Beagle Club held its first national Beagle specialty in many years, in Aldie, Virginia.

1986: The Beagle Brigade, a federal government organization that trains and uses Beagles to sniff out illegal contraband in airports, first formed. Currently, the Beagle Brigade operates under the Department of Homeland Security.

2000: Charles Schulz created the last Peanuts comic strip, and was awarded a Congressional Gold Medal.

Fun Facts

In 2007, Beagles were the fifth most popular breed out of 157 breeds currently recognized by the American Kennel Club. Ironically, the least popular breed, ranked dead last, is the Beagle's cousin, the English Foxhound.

Courtesy of historical information from Dr. Charles Kitchell of Eldridge, Iowa.

What Makes a Beagle?

Beagles hunt rabbits. Many dogs can do the same, so what makes a Beagle a *Beagle?* In large part, a Beagle is a dog that *looks* like a Beagle, and while Beagles don't all look alike, they have certain physical characteristics in common. They also share temperament characteristics. All these qualities add up to "Beagleness," that special something that almost magically translates to the knowledge that the merry little dog on the end of the leash with his nose to the ground is a Beagle.

The Miniature Foxhound

For centuries, people have called the Beagle a "Foxhound in miniature," and the official written breed standard actually uses the term "Miniature Foxhound" to describe the Beagle. A Foxhound is a scent hound that

specializes in chasing foxes. Both breeds have a keen sense of smell, love to chase fast-moving animals, and are friendly with other dogs and people. Given the chance, a Foxhound would probably be happy to chase a rabbit and the Beagle would no doubt enjoy a good run after a fox. Take a look at an English Foxhound and you'll see the resemblance. The Beagle is smaller with shorter legs, but definitely similar—a "Miniature Foxhound."

Beagle Sizes

According to the American Kennel Club, Beagles come in two varieties: 13-inch and 15-inch. The 13-inch Beagle can be up to but not exceed 13 inches tall at the shoulder. The 15-inch variety must be over 13 inches, but not over 15 inches. According to the breed standard, any Beagle over 15 inches tall is disqualified from the show ring. These tall fellows may make fine companions and even good hunters, but they don't conform to the ideal.

The United Kennel Club, a registry that focuses more on hunting dogs than on show dogs, does not divide the Beagle into two varieties. That breed standard simply states that Beagles may not exceed 15 inches in height.

England's Kennel Club also recognizes only one size, which must be at least 13 inches but no more than 16 inches at the shoulder. According to the British breed standard, these minimum and maximum heights are desirable, but falling under or over them is not cause for disqualification.

Although different standards differ slightly, Beagles are, essentially, all between about 13 and 16 inches tall. In other words, they are a small-to-medium dog, big enough to run after rabbits, but not too big to fit in your lap when the day is done.

Beagle Colors and Patterns

The official breed standard states that Beagles may be "any true hound color." But what could that mean? If you look at every breed of hound, you'll see just about every color and pattern known to dogdom: solid-, bi-, or tri-colored, brindled, patched, ticked, mottled, dappled, grizzled, and pied. There is some argument, but generally "any true hound color" means that Beagles should come in the same colors as all the other pack hounds, such as the Foxhounds, the Harriers, and the Basset Hounds.

Breed Truths

One litter of Beagle puppies can contain a whole rainbow of Beagle colors. Classic tri-colored puppies often sit right next to dilute lavender, blue-ticked, and chocolate siblings.

The reason for this standard is to ensure that Beagles haven't been mixed with other breeds. Other colors and patterns might indicate mixing. The various Coonhound breeds, for example, have been mixed with other breeds, creating a wider variety of colors and patterns. Dachshunds and Greyhounds come in colors and patterns that aren't considered traditional on a Beagle. But, as many Beagle enthusiasts like to say, "No good hound can be a bad color." Other aspects of the Beagle are more important.

That said, there are a few commonly recognized Beagle colors and patterns. Beagles are *not* solid-colored; they always have at least two, and not more than three, colors in their coats, always over a white base. Beagles would not be black and tan in the classic Doberman pattern, as this is not considered a "true" hound color. Beagle colors give two options: bi-colored or tri-colored, with the following variations on that theme.

Red and White As you'd expect, red and white beagles are white with patches of reddish brown. The red varies from a light tan (often called lemon-and-white) to a true tan, to clear red to brown to a deeper auburn.

Tri-color Tri-colored Beagles have three different colors in their coats. This usually means a white dog with red patches and a black saddle. Within this category is a good deal

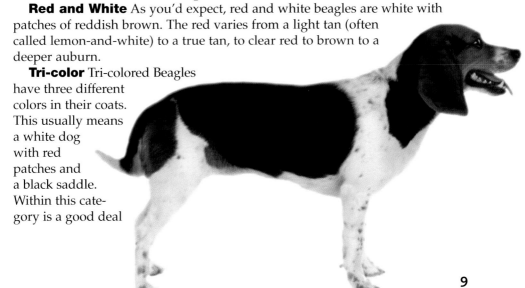

of variation. A classic tri-colored Beagle has a white coat with brown patches and a black saddle over the back, with each color clearly separated from the other. Shaded and faded tri-colored dogs have a smaller, lighter, and/or less defined black saddle, fading into the surrounding color. Tri-colored dogs can also have mottling or ticking over the white areas, as if they were covered in freckles. An open or broken tri-colored dog is mostly white with random, less organized patches of red and black. When the black patches are intermingled with white hairs, the black is sometimes called blue or blue-ticked, but true blue is a dilute black (see below).

Dilute A dilute color is a genetic variation of a color that makes it appear lighter or more faded (diluted). A dark blue tri-color would be a tri-colored dog with dilute black. When the black is diluted to a dark brown, it is called chocolate dilute. When the black is diluted to a lighter brown, it is called liver dilute. These brown-hued dilutes are caused by different genetic factors than the blue dilute. Sometimes dogs have both the blue and chocolate or liver dilute factor, and the result is a color called lilac dilute. The red patches on a Beagle can also be dilute, turning them the light tan or very light lemon colors described previously in the tri-color section. Dogs with the dilute gene usually have perceptibly lighter eyes and lighter-colored noses.

Breed Truths

Although Snoopy is white with black markings, you won't often see a Beagle with that particular pattern. Most Beagles are tri-colored: white with brown and black patches. Bi-colored Beagles are more likely to be white with red markings. Although no rule says a Beagle *can't* be white and black, it isn't very common and would be most likely to occur in Beagles bred for hunting, rather than the show ring.

Pied The pied pattern describes patches over a cream-colored rather than white base. The patches can be light, medium, or dark in color. Badger pied is the darkest, hare pied is the medium shade, and lemon pied is the lightest (dilute) shade. The edges of the patches in a pied Beagle are usually not very clear, as would occur in the faded and shaded patterns described previously in the tri-color section.

Happy Hunters

A Beagle can look exactly like a Beagle, but if he doesn't act like a Beagle, then what's the point? According to the official Beagle breed standard, Beagles should have "the wear-and-tear look of the hound that can last in the chase and follow his quarry to the death," but that's only a part of the true Beagle

spirit. The standard also states that Beagles should "work gaily and cheerfully with flags (tails) up—obeying all commands cheerfully." The British standard puts it succinctly: "A merry hound whose essential function is to hunt, primarily hare, by following a scent. Bold, with great activity, stamina and determination. Alert, intelligent, and of even temperament."

In other words, Beagles are happy hunters, self-confident and cheerful, friendly and ready to work. Those qualities, as much as the floppy ears, soulful eyes, and talented nose, make a Beagle.

The Official Beagle Breed Standard

Once upon a time, there was no Beagle breed standard. "Beagle" was just a name for those happy little hound dogs so good at chasing rabbits. But as dog shows grew in popularity, judges needed something by which to measure the worth of each breed. Today, that measure is the official written breed standard.

In the nineteenth century, breed clubs began forming, each representing a breed. Each has written up very specific guidelines to describe the ideal dog, and while some standards differ from one country to the next or even from one registry to the next (the American Kennel Club standard, for example, is similar but not always identical to the standards of the United Kennel Club, the Canadian Kennel Club, and the English Kennel Club), each very specifically describes what an imaginary, perfect specimen of that breed should be like.

For Beagles in the United States, the breed standard has been written and revised several times by the National Beagle Club. The current standard has been in effect since September 10, 1957, and is officially recognized by the

FYI: What About Puggles?

One of the hottest breeds to hit the pet store circuit in years is the Puggle, a mix between a Pug and a Beagle. Puggles are just one of many "designer dogs" that have resulted from the mixing of two different purebreds. These dogs are the latest fad, but those who work hard to refine a breed and study its history know that it takes a long time to get to a place of reliability and consistency in breeding.

Puggle proponents say these dogs have the very best qualities of both Beagles and Pugs: the Beagle's cheerful friendliness, and the Pug's lower activity level and laid-back attitude. Others say they combine the worst qualities of the two breeds. Pugs are heavy shedders and can be prone to breathing problems and heat exhaustion. Badly-bred Beagles can be hyperactive, and all Beagles tend to be fairly stubborn, selectively-deaf escape artists. A dog that won't listen, begs all the time, and sheds everywhere while panting doesn't seem like the best of both worlds.

That's not to say some Puggles won't make excellent pets. Just keep in mind that any breeder who only gives you the upside of a breed (if Puggles are really a breed) and is eager to get your money without making sure you are going to provide a good permanent home for the dog probably isn't the best source for a pet. For more information on finding a reputable good breeder, see Chapter 3.

If you must have a mixed breed, check out your local animal shelter. Beagle mixes are among the most frequently abandoned of dogs. Why not give one of those lonely guys a second chance instead? For more on adopting a Beagle or Beagle mix, see Chapter 3.

American Kennel Club. While not every Beagle will conform to its exact specifications, it is a standard by which Beagles are typically measured.

Here is the current, official Beagle breed standard, as recognized by the American Kennel Club:

Head

The skull should be fairly long, slightly domed at occiput, with cranium broad and full.

Ears Ears set moderately low, long, reaching when drawn out nearly, if not quite, to the end of the nose; fine in texture, fairly broad—with almost entire absence of erectile power-setting close to the head, with the forward edge slightly inturning to the cheek—rounded at tip.

Eyes Eyes large, set well apart—soft and houndlike—expression gentle and pleading; of a brown or hazel color.

Muzzle Muzzle of medium length, straight and square-cut, the stop moderately defined.

Jaws Level. Lips free from flews; nostrils large and open.

Defects A very flat skull, narrow across the top; excess of dome, eyes small, sharp and terrierlike, or prominent and protruding; muzzle long,

snipy or cut away decidedly below the eyes, or very short. Roman-nosed, or upturned, giving a dish-face expression. Ears short, set on high or with a tendency to rise above the point of origin.

Body

Neck and Throat Neck rising free and light from the shoulders strong in substance yet not loaded, of medium length. The throat clean and free from folds of skin; a slight wrinkle below the angle of the jaw, however, may be allowable.

Defects A thick, short, cloddy neck carried on a line with the top of the shoulders. Throat showing dewlap and folds of skin to a degree termed "throatiness."

Shoulders and Chest Shoulders sloping—clean, muscular, not heavy or loaded—conveying the idea of freedom of action with activity and strength. Chest deep and broad, but not broad enough to interfere with the free play of the shoulders.

Defects Straight, upright shoulders. Chest disproportionately wide or with lack of depth.

Back, Loin and Ribs Back short, muscular and strong. Loin broad and slightly arched, and the ribs well sprung, giving abundance of lung room.

Defects Very long or swayed or roached back. Flat, narrow loin. Flat ribs.

Forelegs Straight, with plenty of bone in proportion to size of the hound. Pasterns short and straight.

Feet Close, round and firm. Pad full and hard.

Defects Out at elbows. Knees knuckled over forward, or bent backward. Forelegs crooked or Dachshundlike. Feet long, open or spreading.

Hips, Thighs, Hind Legs, and Feet Hips and thighs strong and well muscled, giving abundance of propelling power. Stifles strong and well let down. Hocks firm, symmetrical and moderately bent. Feet close and firm.

Defects Cowhocks, or straight hocks. Lack of muscle and propelling power. Open feet.

Tail Set moderately high; carried gaily, but not turned forward over the back; with slight curve; short as compared with size of the hound; with brush.

Defects A long tail. Teapot curve or inclined forward from the root. Rat tail with absence of brush.

Coat A close, hard, hound coat of medium length.

Defects A short, thin coat, or of a soft quality.

Color Any true hound color.

General Appearance A miniature Foxhound, solid and big for his inches, with the wear-and-tear look of the hound that can last in the chase and follow his quarry to the death.

Varieties
There shall be two varieties:

Thirteen Inch—which shall be for hounds not exceeding 13 inches in height.

Fifteen Inch—which shall be for hounds over 13 but not exceeding 15 inches in height.

Disqualification
Any hound measuring more than 15 inches shall be disqualified.

Levelness of Pack
The first thing in a pack to be considered is that they present a unified appearance. The hounds must be as near to the same height, weight, conformation and color as possible.

Individual Merit of the Hounds
Is the individual bench-show quality of the hounds. A very level and sporty pack can be gotten together and not a single hound be a good Beagle. This is to be avoided.

Manners
The hounds must all work gaily and cheerfully, with flags up—obeying all commands cheerfully. They should be broken to heel up, kennel up, follow promptly and stand. Cringing, sulking, lying down to be avoided. Also, a pack must not work as though in terror of master and whips. In Beagle packs it is recommended that the whip be used as little as possible.

FYI: Beagle Cousins

Beagles didn't come out of nowhere. They come from a long and distinguished ancestry of hound dogs, some more closely related than others. Most of the scent hounds were, at one time in history, mixed together, before they were eventually separated out into different breeds with their own breed standards, personalities, and traditions. Here is a look at some of the Beagle's closest cousins.

American Foxhound: A descendant of the English Foxhound, the American Foxhound is descended from dogs that came to America in the seventeenth century, in the company of the colonists. American Foxhounds are pack hunters that hunt fox at high speeds.

Basset Hound: A French descendant of the famous St. Hubert Hounds, the Basset looks like a stockier, shorter, broader Beagle with bigger bones and longer ears. Bassets have also been used throughout their history to trail rabbits and hares at a slower speed, so hunters could follow on foot.

Bloodhound: The leggy Bloodhound also hails from France but is taller, louder, more wrinkled, and—if possible—even more keenly focused on following a scent trail than the Beagle. Bloodhounds are often used by police departments to track human scent trails and they have speed and stamina beyond that of the smaller Beagle.

Dachshund: Long, low, variously coated in smooth hair, long hair, or wirehair, the Dachshund has a unique look and doesn't much resemble the Beagle. However, the two were probably cross-bred frequently in the past. Dachshunds have a slimmer nose and shorter, bowed legs, which a Beagle should not have.

English Foxhound: This is the dog that the Beagle is supposed to resemble, in miniature. However, the Beagle may be older than this breed. Nobody knows for sure. We do know that the English Foxhound and the Beagle do resemble each other, although the English Foxhound is larger, taller, faster, and was designed to hunt fox in hound packs while hunters followed on horseback.

Harrier: Very similar in look to the Beagle, the Harrier is somewhere in size between a Beagle and a Foxhound. Probably descended from French hunting hounds, the Harrier also specializes in hunting hare, more so than rabbits, which are smaller. Harrier can also hunt fox at a pace that allows people to follow on foot.

Appointments

Master and whips should be dressed alike, the master or huntsman to carry horn—the whips and master to carry light thong whips. One whip should carry extra couplings on shoulder strap.

Recommendations for Show Livery

Black velvet cap, white stock, green coat, white breeches or knickerbockers, green or black stockings, white spats, black or dark brown shoes. Vest and gloves optional. Ladies should turn out exactly the same except for a white skirt instead of white breeches.

Chapter Two

The Mind of
the Beagle

What is going on inside that Beagle brain when he cocks his head and looks at you? Is he telling you he likes you, or just trying to con you out of one more treat? Understanding the mind of a Beagle isn't all that difficult. It's just a matter of getting to the bottom of the Beagle's intrinsic character.

In this chapter, you'll get a clearer picture of why Beagles behave the way they do. You'll gain a better understanding of what it means to be a Beagle. You might even achieve a little more patience when faced with how to handle the barking, baying, digging, selectively-deaf, food-obsessed Beagle in *your* life.

Understanding the Beagle Brain

To a Beagle, life isn't that complicated. The world smells amazing, food tastes great, and small, quick, furry things must be chased. Oh, and people can be a lot of fun, too. There's rarely an ulterior motive behind Beagle behavior, unless it's scoring more food or getting closer to a scent trail. Beagles don't try to annoy, frustrate, or one-up their owners and they don't purposefully ignore you or "talk back." They are just being Beagles—cheerful, happy, playful dogs with an absolutely amazing sense of smell . . . and a certain tendency to hyper-focus.

Break down the Beagle universe and take a Beagle's-eye view of each part of it and you'll better understand what those traits mean for you and your efforts to manage your Beagle in the best possible way.

Fun Facts

Humans have about five million scent receptors in their noses, mostly concentrated in one small area in the back. Dogs have close to 200 million of those receptors located all along the nasal passage, and can sense odors at concentrations about 100 million times lower than humans can.

Follow the Nose

When you take your Beagle for a walk, he probably acts like the ground is the most interesting thing he's ever encountered. That's because he can detect—and distinguish between—thousands and thousands of different odors. His sense of smell is so much keener than yours that it's hard to imagine what the world "looks like" to him. A sense of smell that intense can be very distracting.

Humans are visual. Dogs can, of course, *see* things, but their sense of vision isn't nearly as refined as ours (they are, however, particularly good at detecting movement and seeing in low light). So, while humans tend to focus primarily on what they can see, dogs focus primarily on what they can smell.

Some dogs smell better than others. Dogs with longer muzzles generally have more scent receptors than those with shorter snouts and studies have shown that scent hounds, such as Beagles and Bloodhounds, have the best sense of smell, thanks to a big, long muzzle full of scent receptors and sensitive nasal tissues that absorb scent. The Beagles' long ears may also help stir up scent on the ground for even better detection.

Breed Truths

The Beagle's nose surpasses his other skills to such an extent that it really does rule the way he sees (or, smells) the world. Beagles are often described as "stubborn" or "willful" and some owners even feel hurt or offended, believing their Beagle loves food more than he loves his family. That's not exactly true. Your Beagle wants to please you (after all, you smell so good!), but when he gets wind of a really enticing scent, instinct kicks in and there is not much you can do. Don't take it personally. It's not about you. Your Beagle can't help it.

FYI: The "Beagle Brigade"

The Department of Homeland Security Customs and Border Protection doesn't just employ people. Over 1,100 canines help agents track down illegal drugs, explosives, and contraband agricultural products such as meat, fruit, and plants. While larger breeds search airport cargo holds and warehouses, the friendly and unintimidating Beagle is preferred for searching passenger luggage inside airports. The "Beagle Brigade" began in 1984 at Los Angeles International airport with one handler and one Beagle, but quickly expanded. In 2006, 90 agriculture detector dog teams seized 1,145 prohibited agricultural products at ports of entry all over the United States. Good noses!

You can work with your Beagle's amazing scenting ability to benefit both of you. Your voice may not get your Beagle's attention, but a new, exciting smell will. The stinkier the treat, the more likely your Beagle will work to get it. Patience helps, too. Don't scold your Beagle for his all-encompassing focus on a scent trail, but do reward him when he pays attention to you and does what you ask. Food rewards make a lasting impression on a Beagle.

You can also use scent for fun. Bond with your Beagle by playing scent-based games of hide-and-seek. Show him a treat, then hide it and see how long it takes him to find it. Or, get even more serious by learning the fun sport of Tracking (Chapter 7 will tell you more). Understand that to your Beagle, the world really is a giant bouquet of fascinating odors and aromas, and you'll go a long way toward understanding your Beagle.

Chowhound

The Beagle's heightened sense of smell has a side effect: an equally heightened appetite. Beagles love food so much that they will work their hearts out to get it and are notorious food snatchers, counter surfers, and beggars. Some of the Beagle's most ingenious feats and clever displays of reasoning are inspired by food. Beagles also tend to become overweight if their owners pair too many treats with too little exercise.

The Beagle's chowhound nature is to be expected. Working Beagles expend huge amounts of energy hunting, performing, or working in the field, and need to replenish with plenty of food. But even if your Beagle isn't running after rabbits for hours every day, he still has the instinct to chow down.

When food smells so intoxicating, it becomes a great motivator. Use your Beagle's food obsession to your advantage. Dog trainers know that Beagles work best on an empty stomach, when every sensory nerve is attuned to the exact location of something good to eat. Train your Beagle before meal time and you'll get faster results.

Your Beagle's food obsession can get irritating when you wish your dog would focus his attention on you rather than on the biscuit in your pocket,

but don't take this personally. To keep his interest squarely on you, switch out treats often so your Beagle never knows what is hidden in your pocket or behind your back. Always make your Beagle do something to earn any treat or meal you give him, even if it is just to sit nicely first. Your Beagle will quickly learn that he has to earn the stuff he loves the best, and he'll be even more eager to listen to what you want.

Finally, never scold your Beagle for loving food. Just as he can't help following a scent trail, he can't help being a canine gourmand. He can, however, learn not to beg, not to steal, and how to follow the house rules, so set your expectations along those lines and use food to teach your Beagle what you want. Everyone will be happier.

One significant downside to the Beagle's chowhound nature is the tendency to gain too much weight. Many veterinarians say that obesity is the number-one chronic health problem in companion animals today, and Beagles are one of the breeds most prone to this problem. What's so bad about a few extra pounds? When you have a long back, extra weight can put strain on spinal discs and could contribute to a rupture, putting your Beagle at risk for permanent paralysis. Extra fat around internal organs like the heart and lungs makes them have to work harder, making even moderate exercise challenging for your Beagle. Extra weight can also drive up blood sugar, contributing to diabetes, or can exacerbate poor liver or kidney function. As

Helpful Hints

Try these great treats when training your Beagle.

- Tiny bits of lean meat
- Small pieces of lowfat cheese
- Freeze-dried liver
- Blueberries
- Purchased small training treats without fillers or unhealthy additives (look for organic or natural brands)

Beagles age, extra weight puts additional strain on bones and joints, which could make arthritis worse and movement painful.

In other words, too much weight is bad news for Beagles (or anybody, for that matter). Every Beagle should get daily exercise. Young Beagles need a lot of exercise, including the chance to run in a safely fenced area. That leisurely stroll around the block once every evening just isn't enough for an adolescent or young adult Beagle. Daily exercise will help burn off the calories from those beloved treats, but even with exercise, don't overdo the food rewards. Yes, they are effective, but too many treats, too much food, and too many little extras (a slice of bacon here, a piece of cheese there, and wouldn't your Beagle love to drink the milk out of your cereal bowl?) can add a lot of weight fast. Remember, your Beagle depends on you for willpower. He doesn't know he isn't a hunting dog anymore and he can't realize he shouldn't still eat like one. Look away from those pleading eyes, step away from the treats, and go play tag in the backyard instead. (For more information about keeping your Beagle healthy, see Chapter 6.)

Stubborn or Smart?

The Beagle's stubborn streak is legendary. Ask a Beagle to *come* and you may or may not get a response, unless, of course, you are waving a treat in the air. Tell a Beagle to *sit*, and he'll do it if he feels like it. Or not. As for *stay*, well, just hope your Beagle doesn't get wind of something interesting, or he'll forget that he ever learned the meaning of the word.

Your Beagle isn't trying to be cheeky. He simply has more important things to do, and the fact that your every whim isn't necessarily first on his to-do list is more a function of his breeding than his attitude.

To some, the refusal to respond to commands equals stupidity, but Beagles are far from unintelligent. Some breeds are good at responding immediately to cues. Herding and sporting breeds, for instance, are bred to learn very quickly from humans. But remember, Beagles were bred to work without direction from humans. Other than the cue to go hunt and the occasional toot of a horn they were expected to work on their own. Humans have practically demanded that Beagles don't listen too closely to us, so why do we complain so much when they do exactly what we created them to do?

Breed Truths

Beagles are smart, independent, and self-confident, and work best with owners who have those same qualities. Beagles know how to make their own decisions and while they are happy to consider your input, they don't necessarily consider it the law of the land. Consider that independence makes for a more self-sufficient, less needy dog that doesn't require your constant attention to feel secure. Those who don't like clingy, fawning dogs tend to appreciate the Beagle's independence.

The challenge—and the fun—of living with and training a Beagle is figuring out how to keep him interested, motivated, and involved in the decision-making process. Put yourself in his, um . . . paws. If your Beagle figures out for himself that sitting when you give the *sit* command means he will get a treat, then to him, it was all his brilliant idea. Success! For more on good training techniques for Beagles, see Chapter 7.

Managing the One-Beagle Band

Beaglers sometimes call it "singing" or "tongue," but what ever name you give it, Beagles make noise. There is a purpose to this racket. When a Beagle finds a scent trail, he voices his achievement so the hunters know he is on the case. To do this a Beagle needs a loud, musical voice that carries over field and dale.

Your Beagle may not be a hunting dog, but that doesn't mean he's going to keep quiet. He'll let you know if he's hungry or bored or if the mailman is coming or a squirrel has recently run across the property. Beagles will bark or sometimes make a "roo-roo-rooing" sound that can turn into a howl. The moaning wail Beagles make is called "baying," and it's what hound dogs do. You can't train it out of them, and you can't expect to have one of those dogs who rarely makes a noise. It's just not the way Beagles are.

Beagles are not yappy dogs and should not be nuisance barkers. They bark for a reason. However, Beagles can become nuisance barkers if they are left alone all day with nothing to do. The neighbors probably won't appreciate this "music," but to a Beagle, barking is a perfectly reasonable form of entertainment. Beagles aren't born to be backyard loners (arguably, no dog is), and if left to their own devices, they tend to get mouthier than necessary. A bored Beagle is almost certainly a barking Beagle.

The Beagle's lovely singing voice has its upside, too. You'll always know when a stranger approaches, and any barking dog is likely to deter those with bad intentions. Give your Beagle enough exercise, mental challenges, play time, and chew toys, and he should bark, bay, and howl just as much as a Beagle should.

Excessive or nuisance barking is another matter, and can be controlled by keeping the dog inside during distracting times of day (when all the kids in the neighborhood come home from school, for example, or in the evening when people walk their dogs), letting him rest in his crate or

BE PREPARED! Beagles on the Hunt

The Beagle's favorite form of exercise is following a scent trail, so if you have back-yard wildlife, be prepared for your Beagle to be very, very interested. Beagles can get a lot of exercise tracking squirrel, possum, raccoon, and especially rabbit trails around the yard. Some Beagles also consider cats fair game, especially outside. If an animal wanders onto your property, your Beagle will become consumed with the desire to chase, so be sure you have a fence to keep him safe, preferably with an escape route for smaller animals. Confrontations with wildlife can not only get messy, but could injure your Beagle if he gets too close to an animal who wants to fight back. Remember, Beagles are bred to chase rabbits, and rabbits don't normally turn around and bear their teeth and claws.

kennel when guests come over, or simply going out into the yard with him to distract him with fun activities and food treats when he gets too mouthy. Please don't consider de-barking surgery, or even putting a no-bark shock collar on your Beagle. It just isn't fair to expect a Beagle to zip it up. If your Beagle is becoming a nuisance barker, it's probably because you aren't providing him with enough exercise and activities.

On the Move

Some breeds really were bred to lie around. Sight hounds are good at bursts of speed, then days of lounging. Toy breeds are particularly adept at resting quietly on laps or in handbags. Some extra-large working dogs like to laze around too, until they are called to guard property or pull a cart.

COMPATIBILITY Is a Beagle the Best Breed for You?

ENERGY LEVEL	● ● ●
EXERCISE REQUIREMENTS	● ● ●
PLAYFULNESS	● ● ● ●
AFFECTION LEVEL	● ● ●
FRIENDLINESS TOWARD OTHER PETS	● ● ● ●
FRIENDLINESS TOWARD STRANGERS	● ● ●
FRIENDLINESS TOWARD CHILDREN	● ● ● ●
EASE OF TRAINING	● ●
GROOMING EFFORT	●
SHEDDING	● ● ●
SPACE REQUIREMENTS	● ●
OK FOR BEGINNERS	● ● ● ●

4 Dots = Highest rating on scale

Not Beagles. This breed needs to move. Throughout their history, Beagles have had to spend endless hours running after a scent trail. They had to have great endurance and be true athletes: strong, coordinated, and energetic. Deny them the chance to fulfill their genetic destiny, and you are asking for trouble. Couch-potato Beagles become overweight. Beagles aren't made to lounge around all day. They are made to run and run some more, with no thought to anything else, in pursuit of a smell.

If you don't provide your Beagle with enough opportunities for exercise, he will find other ways to get all that energy out of his system. He may dig up the yard or dig under the fence and run off to find something more interesting to do. He may start barking and howling, purely out of boredom. Chewing is a perfectly reasonable form of entertainment for a dog, and when there is nothing else to do, he'll look for the best candidates: your shoes, your child's favorite teddy bear, or your pillow.

Fun Facts

When Snoopy first appeared in the *Peanuts* cartoon strip in 1950, he walked on four legs like any other Beagle. On January 5, 1956, Snoopy stood upright—and has ever since.

Beagles need long walks, active playtime, training sessions, and time in the dog park, if you have access to one. Don't skip a day. Well-exercised Beagles are much less likely to engage in unwanted behaviors. They will behave more calmly and be nicer in the house, they won't make as much noise, and they won't destroy things (at least after the puppy teething stage is over).

Plus, Beagle owners often find that they get more exercise when they walk and play with their dogs every day. Keeping your Beagle on the move may benefit you, too. For more on great ways to exercise your Beagle, see Chapter 7.

Family Friend

A Beagle who picks fights with other dogs wouldn't last very long in a pack situation and he wouldn't make a good hunting dog if he was aggressive toward humans, either. For that reason Beagles have cheerful, agreeable temperaments and consider most people and other dogs to be friends unless they prove themselves otherwise. Beagles also have a special sensitivity for children and those who are sick, injured, or elderly. While there are exceptions, well-socialized Beagles understand how to be gentle with people who need a softer approach, and are rarely provoked to bite unless seriously threatened.

In other words, Beagles make great family friends. Just don't make the mistake of thinking yours will automatically love everybody without any work on your part. Your Beagle needs to be socialized from early puppyhood,

PERSONALITY POINTERS
Beagle Body Language

Beagle Mood	Friendly	Interested or Excited	Playful
Head Carriage	Normal posture and head position	Normal posture and head position	"Play bow," chest and head lowered to ground, head looking up
Eyes	Wide open	Wide open	Wide open
Ears	Alert, forward	Alert, forward	Alert, forward
Mouth	Closed or relaxed, some "smile"	Open, teeth covered with lips, sometimes panting	Closed or slightly open, lips covered
Body	Relaxed, wiggling	Relaxed, wiggling, moving forward	Chest lowered to ground, rump elevated
Tail	Wagging	Wagging	Wagging

meeting lots of friendly people and other pets in a variety of situations. If your Beagle puppy experiences the world as a friendly and welcoming place, he'll be a better judge of character as an adult.

Take your Beagle to puppy classes and adult training classes, travel with him, and bring him on errands around town (don't leave him in the car). Let him play with children and other dogs, but also be his protector. A bad experience with an unfriendly person, rough child, or aggressive dog could have an antisocializing effect, turning your Beagle into an overly shy dog, or even a dog who bites out of fear.

Beagles love children, and have a reputation for being great "kid dogs." Kids and Beagles are a perfect match, with proper adult supervision. Most kids have more energy than adults, so they can play longer. Beagles are small enough not to overwhelm a child, and many children learn basic dog training and even dog showing with Beagles, who love to do what their little "siblings" ask of them—especially if they have treats. Beagles are wise

Apprehensive or Anxious	Submissive	Fearful	Dominant
Neck stiff, head may be pulled back slightly	Head slightly lowered, looking down	Head slightly lowered, looking down or away	Head slightly forward, facing squarely
Wide open or bug-eyed with whites of eyes showing	Eyes partially closed	Eyes white, whites of eyes showing	Staring
Pulled back	Flattened against the skull	Pulled back or flattened	Forward
Closed or slightly open with lips pulled tight, teeth showing	Lips pulled back, tense "smile," licking, panting, or nuzzling to pacify	Slightly open, showing teeth, might drool, lick, or pant	Lips tight, showing teeth, may curl lip or growl
Tense, stiff	Tense, stiff, or may roll over on the back or urinate submissively	Tense, may tremble or back away	Leaning forward, stiff legged, advancing, putting paws on another dog's neck or back
Lowered or partially lowered	Lowered, tucked between legs	Lowered or tucked	Raised, held stiff, may quiver or even wag

to the fact that most of the food gets spilled by the kids (especially the ones in the high chairs). Beagles and children have a lot in common: high energy, a good sense of humor, a sense of wonder about the world, and the ability to concentrate almost exclusively on something really interesting.

Growing up with a Beagle can be great for kids, too. Living with a dog—with appropriate adult supervision and guidance—teaches a child how to be kind to animals, respect other living creatures, and even take on some personal responsibility by helping out with the Beagle's care. However, no child should ever be solely responsible for a Beagle, and getting rid of the dog should never be a punishment for failure to meet those responsibilities. The adult must be in charge and make sure the Beagle gets food, exercise, and loving attention every day. Some kids may be able to remember to feed, train, and groom a Beagle, but many simply aren't mature enough to do these jobs in a responsible or reliable way. Make no mistake: It's *your Beagle,* even if you say the Beagle belongs to your child. It's only fair to the dog.

10 Questions About Beagles

1 Do Beagles really need a fenced yard? Either you take your Beagle on a couple of long brisk walks every day on a leash without fail, or you're going to need a fenced yard. Beagles need a lot of exercise, and because they will follow a scent trail or a fast-moving animal without regard for hazards like oncoming cars, a fence is a necessity.

2 Why is my Beagle constantly making noise? Beagles are bred to raise a racket. If they don't bark, bay, whine, howl, or generally carry on, how will the hunter know the pack is on the trail? You can't train your Beagle to be silent. Instead, concentrate on giving your Beagle enough exercise and attention that he doesn't become a nuisance barker out of boredom.

3 Are Beagles hyperactive? A well-bred Beagle should not be naturally hyperactive, but a Beagle bred with no regard for a good temperament might be. Some smaller Beagles tend to be more hyperactive than larger Beagles, but there are many exceptions. That said, Beagles are very high-energy dogs. If they don't get enough exercise, interaction, and attention from you, they probably will seem hyperactive.

4 Are Beagles hard to housetrain? Beagles are easier to housetrain than some breeds, harder than others. Look for signs he needs to go (sniffing, circling) and consistently take him out every few hours. He'll learn quickly. Crate training works, too.

5 Are Beagles hard to obedience train? Beagles like to please, but their independent nature—a function of centuries of breeding to work alone in the field—can make them an obedience challenge. However, any Beagle can learn basic rules and good manners in the house, especially in a basic obedience class.

6 Will a Beagle like my kids? Are your kids nice? Do they know how to play appropriately with a dog? Do they like to throw a ball? Do they like to play chase, tag, and dress-up? Would they never even think of poking eyes or pulling tails? Then what's not to like?

7 Does my Beagle like food better than he likes me? Some pet owners can feel downright dissed when their Beagles seem more interested in the treat in the hand than the owner of the hand, but the Beagle has such a finely-tuned sense of smell that aromas really do seem to switch off the other parts of his brain. But food is a tool, not a competitor for your Beagle's affection. If you are the magical source of those fantastic treats, your Beagle will be very motivated to do just about anything you ask.

8 Do I have to worry about my Beagle getting fat? Yes. Beagles like food so much that they don't always realize when they should stop eating. Monitor your Beagle's food and treat intake and dial it back if your Beagle begins to resemble a sausage more than a sleek hunting dog.

9 Do Beagles stink? Beagles do not normally have that notorious musky hound-dog smell, but a Beagle who's rolled in something delightfully stinky will need a bath.

10 Do I really have to exercise my Beagle every day? Yes. Without exercise, Beagles can become destructive, nuisance barkers, hyperactive, and dangerously overweight. Besides, it's good for you, too.

Chapter Three

How to Choose a Beagle

S o you've decided that you really do have the desire, the motivation, and the resources to live happily with a Beagle? Great. The next step is to find a good one.

Popularity has its downside. Beagles are easy to find, but one of the unfortunate side effects of the Beagle's "fifth-most-popular-breed-in-America" status is that finding a good Beagle from a responsible, ethical breeder isn't so easy. Because there's a profit to be made from breeding Beagles (or so-called "designer dog" Beagle mixes, like Puggles), unscrupulous types often breed dogs in volume with no regard to improving, or even maintaining, good genetic health, the right Beagle look, or even the good temperament so essential for a successful family pet. When money is the bottom line, Beagles and pet owners often lose.

The family down the street with a litter of Beagle pups may not be the best source for a Beagle, even if the pups are "free to a good home." People who breed for fun, or by accident, usually don't know much about dog breeding, canine genetics, or the finer points of temperament. You may get a good family pet from a source like this, but you are taking a risk. Will the puppies grow up to look and act like Beagles? Maybe. Or maybe not.

If you really want to maximize your chances for getting a healthy Beagle that looks and acts like a Beagle, your best bet is to find a reputable and experienced hobby breeder. Or, if you are open to an older dog, consider adopting a Beagle from an animal shelter or pet rescue group.

Beagle Sources

Before diving into the finer points of great Beagle breeders, let's consider some of the most common sources for pets, and why they aren't such a great idea. While you might find a great Beagle from any of these sources, chances are relatively high that you will end up with problems. Those problems might take the form of health issues and high veterinarian bills, temperament problems, or a dog that grows up barely resembling a Beagle.

CHECKLIST

Are You Ready for a Beagle?

Are you ready for a Beagle? Don't answer "yes!" until you can confidently check everything on this list.

✔ I understand that hound dogs are obsessed with smells, so I know to keep my Beagle on a leash or safely within a fenced yard at all times.

✔ I am ready to play second fiddle to food of any kind.

✔ I am fully prepared to give my Beagle vigorous daily exercise.

✔ I realize my Beagle may not always listen to me, or do what I say, at least not the first time.

✔ I am prepared to take my Beagle puppy to puppy training classes, and after that, to enroll him in a basic obedience class with a trainer who focuses on positive reinforcement training methods.

✔ I know Beagles shed. I also know how to brush my Beagle every few days to minimize this. Besides, I don't mind a little Beagle hair on my clothes and furniture.

✔ I know Beagles need socialization, so I will take my Beagle out in the world and introduce him to many different people, places, and other animals, in a safe way. I want my Beagle to be a good citizen and understand how life in the human world works for a good dog.

✔ I will use small, healthy treats for more effective training.

✔ I will spend time with my Beagle every day. After all, that's why I want a Beagle.

Of course you'll want your Beagle as soon as possible, but take the time to consider where you buy your puppy, and be sure your source is a good one. You'll be making an investment that will pay back many times over.

Pet Stores

A pet store may be the first source that comes to mind when you are thinking of buying a puppy. After all, it seems the logical place to go. However, if you can't see the parents of the litter or meet the breeder, you can't know what kind of conditions the puppies in the store came from, what the parents look like, or how the puppies will act. A pet store doesn't often afford you the luxury of meeting your pup's parents or his breeder, and although they might be great, you won't know for sure. So try to investigate the store and its reputation. Make sure to ask for all certification papers and medical records. You can never be too careful.

Pet stores are awfully convenient, which is tempting to those who want instant gratification. But impulse buying is the worst way to buy a dog. Remember, the pet you are purchasing will be part of your family for the next 12 to 15 years.

FYI: Leaving the Litter

According to veterinarians and animal behaviorists, puppies shouldn't leave the litter until they are at least 7 or 8 weeks old. Some breeders insist on keeping puppies with their mothers and litter-mates until 10 or even 12 weeks. This extra time lets puppies nurse longer for good immune support and also helps them feel secure and safe. Puppies go through several crucial developmental stages in the company of their mother and littermates. Interfering with this natural development can cause temperament troubles later.

Neighbors

So the family down the street has a Beagle who got frisky on a play date, or spent an unfortunate night on the town? Sometimes, a Beagle puppy practically falls into your lap, and that can be a fine way to bring a Beagle into your home. However, be sure you realize the risks you take when you get a Beagle from someone who didn't necessarily plan a breeding.

Do you know what both the parents look like, or did the Beagle just come home pregnant after escaping from the yard? Do you know if both parents were really Beagles, and if not, do you know what other breeds might be involved? Nothing against mixed breeds, but it helps to know if your puppy is going to grow up to weigh more than you do, or will just fit in your pocket.

Even more importantly, do you know the temperaments of both parents? If that pretty female Beagle got involved with a thug of questionable character (or maybe the female involved was the troublemaker), the puppies could inherit the less desirable traits of the errant parent.

Temperament is partly influenced by how a dog is socialized and trained, but it is also genetic. If you don't know the history of one of the parents, you may be in for a surprise. (Have you ever seen a 24-inch Beagle? Or a Beagle with a guard-dog instinct? Or long hair?). Maybe the risk is worthwhile to you, and if you are willing to care for, train, and pay attention to the dog throughout his whole life, no matter what he grows into, then that's great. Just go into the situation with both eyes open. Just because a dog was cheap or free doesn't mean it's okay to throw him away if he doesn't work out exactly the way you planned.

CAUTION

Beagle puppies are adorable and hard to resist, but without seeing the parents, you can't be sure that your cute little bundle of fur won't grow up too big (or too small), or with other features that don't much resemble a Beagle. If you can't meet the parents, think long and hard about whether you are really willing to take the risk and buy that Beagle.

Newspaper and Internet Ads

Whether you see an ad for a Beagle that is "free to a good home" or a "breeder of champions," be a little wary. Most reputable breeders have waiting lists for their puppies and don't need to advertise in newspapers. While some of these breeders have web sites, they aren't usually willing to sell a puppy via the Internet without carefully interviewing the buyer and preferably meeting him or her in person. Breeders more interested in Beagles than in profits don't want their little puppies to go just anywhere. They want to be sure they have good homes for life.

If the ad looks really promising, check it out. Make a call and pay a visit to the home or breeding facility. Bring a list of questions, and see how it goes. Maybe you've found a gem, but if you recognize any of the red flags mentioned in this chapter, don't hand over the cash or take home the dog.

Auctions and Flea Markets

If you see a box of puppies at an auction or flea market, you can bet the seller is in it for the money. This impulse to "rescue" them is perfectly understandable, but, if you hand over your hard-earned cash to the seller, you are essentially saying "Keep doing this because it pays." Most of the dogs in these situations were bred in less than ideal conditions, as a commodity. Sure, you feel sorry for them. We all do. But sending the message that this kind of practice is okay does more harm than good. Step back and think before you act.

If you see a box of puppies in front of a supermarket or anywhere else in public, you should also be wary. Maybe somebody is just trying to get rid of an accidental litter, but if you can't see the parents, it's buyer beware. Are you ready to commit to that dog and not give it away at the first sign that it isn't the Beagle you thought it would be? Know the risk and go in with both eyes open.

CAUTION

It's never a good idea to buy or agree to take any puppy or dog without seeing it first, unless you already know and trust the breeder from previous experience. Less reputable sellers may pull the old "bait and switch," telling you that you will get one dog, then giving you another one they would rather get rid of. Some may try to convince you to take a puppy they know is unhealthy at a cheaper price, hoping you won't do anything about it, or will never be the wiser. Be the wiser and don't get into that situation in the first place.

Hobby Breeders

Fortunately, there are plenty of excellent, ethical hobby breeders out there, working hard to improve the health, temperament, and beauty of the Beagle breed. These breeders want the very best for their beautiful pups. They plan breedings carefully, test the parents for genetic health issues to minimize the chance for passing along disease, and they handle the puppies from birth to socialize them to humans.

Good breeders know each puppy's personality and can help you choose the puppy with the right temperament for you and your situation. They will be there when you have questions, and can serve as a valuable resource for the rest of that dog's life.

Good hobby breeders don't typically make much, if any, profit. Most of the money they earn on a Beagle puppy goes toward genetic testing, veterinary visits, high quality food and supplies, and the breeder's valuable time working with and socializing the puppies. Spending your money on this kind of Beagle is voting with your dollars for what's in the best interest of Beagles.

The best source for good Beagle breeders is the National Beagle Club of America (NBC). This American Kennel Club-recognized national breed club lists member breeders—who are involved in dog shows, field trials, pack hunting, competitive obedience, agility, and other dog sports—and who are committed to breeding the very best Beagles. These breeders aren't breeding for profit, but for the love of Beagles and the desire to bring better and better Beagles into the world—dogs with great temperaments who can excel in dog shows or in that breeder's chosen sport, and who could still fulfill the functions the Beagle was born to fulfill (namely, hunting rabbits).

Not every good hobby breeder is a member of the NBC, but almost every good hobby breeder is a member of some kind of club, such as a local breed or sporting club. The American Kennel Club lists many kinds of local as well as national breed clubs on their web site, such as national clubs, agility clubs, local conformation (dog show) clubs, performance clubs, tracking clubs, and training clubs.

Good hobby breeders show their dogs in dog shows, hunt with their dogs in packs, or train and compete with their dogs in sports like obedience or agility, so when you are screening breeders, be sure to ask what kinds of activities they do with their dogs.

Finding a Breeder

When you have a list of a few potential breeders (or even if you've only found one), the first step is to make phone calls. Call the breeder and have a conversation. You should be able to tell a lot from a phone call.

A good breeder will want to know some information about you. This isn't an invasion of your privacy, it is evidence that the breeder cares about his puppies and wants to screen out inappropriate homes. If the breeder doesn't ask you questions but immediately invites you out to buy a puppy, consider that a red flag.

When evaluating a breeder, consider the following. You can also take the opportunity to ask the breeder some important questions.

- Are the puppies immediately available? Breeders who always have a constant supply of puppies are probably breeding for profit. Good hobby breeders usually only breed one or two litters a year at most, and many have a waiting list. Your breeder may know of other breeders with puppies currently available, and may be able to refer you, but *when* a puppy is available should be less of a consideration than the quality of the puppies and the breeder.
- Are the Beagles bred for the show ring, hunting, or field trials? Breeders who show their dogs in conformation dog shows typically have attractive Beagles with good, calm temperaments suitable for pet homes. Breeders who breed dogs for hunting, field trials, or competitive sports may have higher-energy dogs that vary more in appearance but are good competitors in dog sports or natural trackers, although this isn't necessarily true. Breeders who don't do anything with their dogs are probably breeding for profit.

If you want a hunting dog, it's a good idea to get a Beagle from a hunting kennel that can advise you, and that breeds for the qualities necessary in a good hunting dog. If you are interested

Helpful Hints

A few good places to find reputable hobby breeders:

- Visit the National Beagle Club's breeder referral page: *http://clubs.akc.org/NBC/ breeders_list.htm.*
- Contact local breed or training clubs for referrals. Find them on the American Kennel Club "club search" web page at *http://www.akc.org/clubs/search/ index.cfm*, or look in the phone book under "dog clubs" or "dog training."
- Ask local obedience instructors about good Beagle breeders in the area.
- Ask your veterinarian if she knows any good, responsible Beagle breeders.
- Visit dog shows in your area and talk to the people exhibiting the Beagles (but wait until they are finished in the ring!).

FYI: National Beagle Club

Every breeder who belongs to the National Beagle Club must agree to do the following

1. Abide by the by-laws and policies of the National Beagle Club of America, Inc., and the rules of the American Kennel Club.
2. Provide the best possible standard of health and care for the animals, including regular veterinary examinations, vaccinations, proper nutrition, and housing.
3. Not engage in and discourage indiscriminate breeding of dogs.

4. Refuse to breed any animal in poor health, of unsound temperament, or having known hereditary show-disqualifying faults.
5. Refuse to raffle dogs or to sell individuals or litter lots to pet wholesalers, laboratories, pet shops, or any buyer who will not provide proper care for the puppy or dog.

The NBC considers the violation of any of these principles to be grounds for expulsion from the breed club.

in pursuing competitive agility, a breeder who has high-drive, athletic dogs might be more appropriate than a show breeder. If you want a dog with a calm, steady temperament to be a good family pet, a show breeder who breeds dogs to be calm in the busy show ring might be perfect. In other words, your priorities for your dog should match the breeder's priorities.

- Where are the dogs housed? Good hobby breeders usually raise their puppies inside the house, where they can be in contact with humans. Some keep their adult dogs in the house, others keep them in comfortable, clean kennel facilities.
- Have the parents been tested for genetic disorders? Reputable hobby breeders typically test their Beagles for common genetic diseases, like hip dysplasia, glaucoma, and progressive retinal atrophy (a degenerative eye disease) and should be willing to share the test results with you. Good breeders will include a written health guarantee protecting you and the breeder (the breeder can't be responsible for health problems that occur because of buyer negligence).
- Are the parents on the premises? A reputable breeder will typically let you see the mother of the litter, so you can see how the puppies are likely to look and what kind of temperament they are likely to have. The father or "sire" may live with another breeder, but you should at least be able to see pictures of him, or get the contact information for the sire's owner so you can find out more about his look and temperament.
- Are references available? If the breeder won't give you any, or says he does all his own vaccinations and care on-site and doesn't need a veterinarian, walk away.

BE PREPARED! Ten Questions to Ask the Breeder

1. How old are the pups and what colors, sexes, and ages are available?

2. Are the parents of the pups registered with a recognized kennel club, such as the American Kennel Club?

3. Have the pups been examined and vaccinated by a veterinarian? If so, which vaccinations have the pups received? Do the pups have any special health certifications from veterinary specialists?

4. How many pups are in the litter and at what age were they weaned?

5. Have the pups been treated or tested for internal and external parasites?

6. Does the breeder keep track of and test for health problems? Are there any known health problems in the puppy's family lines?

7. Have the pups received any basic training, including housetraining, crate training, or leash training?

8. What kind of food do the pups eat? How much and how often do they eat?

9. Can you see the parents and littermates of the pup and the environment where the puppies are raised?

10. Will the breeder take the dog back if at some time you are unable to care for him?

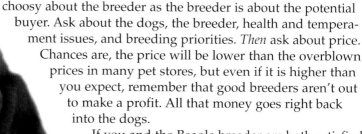

Don't begin your conversation with the breeder by asking about price. Good breeders don't want to give their puppies to people who are most concerned with getting a cheap deal. They are looking for people who are as choosy about the breeder as the breeder is about the potential buyer. Ask about the dogs, the breeder, health and temperament issues, and breeding priorities. *Then* ask about price. Chances are, the price will be lower than the overblown prices in many pet stores, but even if it is higher than you expect, remember that good breeders aren't out to make a profit. All that money goes right back into the dogs.

If you and the Beagle breeder are both satisfied with what you hear on the phone, it's time to pay a visit in person. Even if you have to drive for a few hours, visiting the breeder is crucial for determining whether or not you really are working with someone reputable.

When you arrive at the breeder's home or kennel, keep your eyes open. Although many breeders are just as

BE PREPARED! Questions the Breeder Will Ask You

1. Why do you want a Beagle? What do you want or expect from your Beagle? What are your plans for him?

2. Do you have experience with Beagles, or have you owned a Beagle in the past?

3. Do you have the necessary time and money to properly care for a Beagle now and in the long-range future?

4. What kind of home can you provide? (Note: Beagles should be housed indoors only unless they are part of a hunting pack kept in comfortable outdoor housing with other dogs.)

5. Do you have other pets or children in the home? If so, what type of pets and how old are the children?

6. Do you have a fenced-in yard, patio, or safe enclosure for a Beagle?

7. How many hours a day are you home? Do you have time to care for your Beagle, including playtime and daily walks?

8. Can you provide the name and phone number of your veterinarian for a reference and follow-up contact?

9. Can the breeder meet all members of your family who will be living with the Beagle?

10. Do you plan to take your Beagle with you on trips and vacations? If not, who will care for your Beagle while you are away?

11. Do you promise to contact the breeder immediately in the event that you are no longer able to keep or care for your Beagle?

good as they sound on the phone, some talk the talk but don't deliver when you visit in person. Kennels should be clean, dogs should look happy and healthy, and you should not be greeted by any aggression (from Beagles or the breeder!). Beagles bark, but they bark out of a cheerful optimism that you are certainly a new friend, not out of some misguided notion that they are attack dogs or you have come to harm them.

Ask questions and request to see one or both parents. You should feel comfortable with the breeder, and have the impression that he is trustworthy and not trying to trick you into anything. Most importantly, you should pay attention to the dogs. If they look and behave the way you would like your own Beagle to look and behave, that's a good sign.

Red Flags

When you really want a dog, it can be tempting to overlook some red flags at the breeder. However, you will be better off paying attention to signs of trouble than ignoring them and paying the price later. If you detect any of the following, either on the phone or in person when talking to or visiting the breeder, proceed with caution and find out more. Or, say "Thanks but no thanks," and keep looking.

- The kennel or home is noticeably filthy.
- The Beagles on the premises look mangy, dirty, or sickly.
- The Beagles on the premises act desperate or aggressive, rather than friendly.
- Young puppies are raised outside.
- The breeder has many different breeds, rather than specializing in just one or two.
- The breeder has a large number of dogs and many kennels. This isn't always a red flag, but it can be a sign of a for-profit, volume breeder.
- The breeder tries to get you to buy a Beagle right away.
- The breeder tries to convince you to take on a small or sickly Beagle at a "reduced price."
- The breeder sells "Pocket Beagles" or has some other name for extremely small Beagles, at a higher price. Remember, the little ones aren't more valuable, but they are more likely to have health problems and should never cost more than properly-sized, healthy Beagle pups.
- The breeder gives you conflicting information from what was said on the phone.
- The breeder doesn't show, hunt, or compete with his dogs.
- The breeder refuses to show you the parents or has an excuse about how the dam "isn't there right now." (Ask to come back when you can see the mother.)
- The breeder won't let you interact with any of the dogs.
- The breeder won't give you any references from former buyers or veterinarians.
- The breeder's puppies aren't eligible for registration, or are eligible, but through a registry other than a reputable one you have heard of, like the American Kennel Club (AKC) or the United Kennel Club (UKC). Some registries will register any dog, as long as the breeder pays a fee, without any regard to the true purebred nature or pedigree of the dog. Some registries have acronyms that sound *like* AKC or UKC, so get the full name of the registry.

Choosing the Perfect Beagle Puppy

When you've found someone you feel great about, the next step is to pick your puppy, or get on a waiting list so you can pick your puppy when he is born. Either way, you'll eventually need to decide which puppy is the one for you.

Good breeders have been handling the puppies since birth. They want to evaluate what dogs are promising for the show ring, the field trial, the

hunting pack, the obedience ring, or any other relevant Beagle activities. As the breeder evaluates the puppies, she also notices which ones don't quite fit her needs, but would make great pets. Part of that evaluation is determining the different puppy temperaments: which ones are a little bolder, a little more laid-back, a little cautious. Breeders can tell the daredevils from the wallflowers, and they know exactly what kind of homes would be best for each of those puppies and their individual personalities.

This is one of the reasons why the breeder asks you so many questions. Once she determines you are a good potential Beagle parent, she wants to figure out exactly which Beagle would work best for you. In other words, let the breeder help you choose a puppy.

Helpful Hints

You may have heard about temperament testing, health evaluation, and other ways to choose the perfect pup, but the simple fact is that if you have found a responsible, reputable breeder, all the puppies will probably be healthy and have good temperaments. As for the minute differences in temperament between puppies, nobody knows those puppies better than the observant hobby breeder.

PERSONALITY POINTERS
Puppy Aptitude Test*

Test/Purpose	How to Test
Social Attraction Measures sociability and interest in people.	Coax the puppy to come to you.
Following Measures interest in people and dependence versus independence.	Get the puppy's attention, then walk away from the puppy.
Restraint Measures dominance versus submissiveness.	Gently roll the puppy on his back and hold him there.
Social Dominance Measures the puppy's willingness to interact with people.	Stroke the puppy on the back while the puppy is in a standing position.
Elevation Dominance Tests how the puppy responds to being held in the air, which is a measure of trust in people.	Lift the puppy slightly off the ground and hold it there.
Retrieving Measures the instinctive response to retriever.	Toss a crumpled-up piece of paper in front of the puppy.
Sound Sensitivity Measures sensitivity to loud or unfamiliar noises	Make a sharp noise, such as a clap, or drop something on the floor, a few feet from the puppy.
Touch Sensitivity Measures sensitivity to being handled	Gently press the webbing between the puppy's toes.
Sight Sensitivity Measures visual sensitivity to moving and unfamiliar objects.	Tie a string to a towel, then wave the towel near the puppy.

*Try these tests on the puppy you are thinking about buying. Traditionally used to choose candidates for guide dog training programs, these tests can help to predict a puppy's personality. They aren't always right, but they can help you make a choice.

What to Look For	Results
Does the puppy come eagerly, eventually, not at all, or does the puppy run away, back away, or cower?	The faster the puppy comes, the more sociable and confident the puppy may grow up to be.
Does the puppy follow eagerly, hesitatingly, not at all, or does he run the other way?	The more eagerly the puppy follows, the more dependent he is, but in a good way. Puppies that are too independent don't listen well and can be harder to train.
Does the puppy fight and struggle, move at first but then relax, or immediately give up and lie limp or submissively urinate?	Look for a puppy to struggle at first but then relax. Too much fighting means a dog may be strong-willed, but fear during this test may indicate lack of confidence.
Does the puppy protest, run away, lick the tester, or roll over immediately?	A puppy that enjoys and responds to petting is ideal. Running away or rolling over are signs that the puppy is not interested in or is afraid of people.
Does the puppy struggle fiercely, hang out like it is no big deal, lick, or freeze and act frightened?	Look for a confident but laid-back response. Struggling fiercely or fearful licking or freezing are signs that the puppy has problems accepting your leadership.
Does the puppy fetch it, grab it and run away, or ignore it?	A puppy that runs after the paper and brings it back is a good prospect for sports that require retrieving. A puppy that ignores the paper may be more difficult to train.
Does the puppy bark, look interested, or cringe and shy away?	Interest without fear is best.
How long does it take the puppy to protest?	The puppy should not be scared or startled but may get annoyed after a few seconds.
Does the puppy chase or try to play with the towel, just look, ignore the towel, or back up or cower?	The puppy that looks interested but isn't threatened or aggressive to the towel is the best choice.

You may fall in love with the rambunctious one constantly climbing out of the whelping box to conquer the world, but he won't be a good fit if you are a laid-back type who would eventually get tired of the constant high-energy needs of an extra-active Beagle. You may want a running buddy and be best suited to the puppy who has potential to be a real athlete. If you want a dog that will be good with kids, seniors, or cats or fit into a busy household, the breeder can advise you.

Sometimes, fate takes over and you just *know* a certain dog is yours. But if you have any doubts, or can't decide, or aren't quite sure, or even if you think you know exactly which puppy you need to bring into your family, let the breeder lead the way. She could help you avoid making a mistake you'll regret later.

Second-hand Beagles

Some potential dog owners think they want a Beagle, then quickly discover they can't handle the hound. As a result many Beagles are abandoned to shelters and rescue groups. Many more Beagle mixes wait in shelters for someone to give them a home. It's a sad situation, and if you'd like to do something about it, consider adopting a shelter or rescued Beagle.

Second-hand dogs aren't for everyone. You will have to be willing to accept the following:

- Most rescues aren't puppies.
- Most rescues will need a little extra time and patience to settle in.
- Some rescues have behavioral or health problems that must be addressed.

However, rescuing a Beagle also has some definite perks

- Since most rescues are adult dogs, there will likely be no housetraining, chewing, or crazy puppy antics to deal with.
- Many rescues already have basic obedience training and know how to live nicely inside the house with you.
- Beagles are an adaptable breed and many quickly adjust to new homes and new families who give them enough exercise and attention.

Rescue groups spend a lot of time getting to know the dogs that come in, and most can give you information about the dog's behavioral traits. For instance, tests may have been done to determine whether a dog is good with children, with other dogs, and with cats. They may also be able to tell you something about the Beagle's past, if they have that information. And, they will want to know all about you, to be sure you won't end up dumping the dog again.

If you think rescuing a Beagle might be for you, visit local shelters and contact local rescue groups.

Animal Shelters

Most cities have animal shelters, either run by the city or by a local humane society or other privately-run group. Typically, city-run or county-run shelters take in any animals that are abandoned, including those they pick up off the streets. Privately-run shelters may be choosier, so they don't have to euthanize any animals. They may take in only animals they think are adoptable.

If you find a dog at an animal shelter that you want to adopt, you will have to fill out an application. Many shelters want to know where you will keep your Beagle, how often you are home, and other details about your life. They aren't being nosy. They just want to be sure the Beagle is going to a good—and *permanent*—home. Many shelters also have some stipulations, such as

- A 24-hour waiting period to review your application and to make sure you don't have second thoughts about your decision.
- Refusal to place animals with college students. Some shelters have a no-exceptions policy to this rule. They've simply seen too many students abandon pets at the end of the school year.
- Landlord's permission if you are a renter. The shelter wants to be sure you aren't keeping the animal illegally, which could result in surrendering the animal if you are ever found out.

Many shelter adoptions turn out beautifully. Adopted Beagles somehow seem to know you've given them a second chance, and seem eternally grateful and especially bonded to the people who take them in.

Sometimes, however, shelter adoptions don't work out. You find out things about the animal that you didn't know upon adoption, such as a tendency to bite or being afraid of children or anything else that makes the situation unworkable. For all concerned, it is almost always best if you work out problems because no dog needs to lose a home multiple times, but

reality being what it is, there are exceptions. To help minimize this risk, if you have any doubts about the dog you want to adopt, wait. There will always be more Beagles and Beagle mixes needing rescue.

Beagle Rescue

Beagle rescue groups are a lot different than animal shelters. For starters, they specialize in Beagles only, and some only take purebred Beagles. Second, they are privately run, usually solely by volunteers, and usually don't have a facility. Beagles that come into the rescue groups usually live with volunteer "foster parents" until the group can find good homes for them.

Helpful Hints

Shelter workers are often overworked and underpaid, but they generally do their best to make sure adoptable animals are placed into good homes, when possible. Pay a visit. See what your shelter is like. Find out how much evaluation they do for adoptable animals. Ask questions, and browse the kennels, looking for Beagles. You may change your mind about "needing" a purebred Beagle puppy.

Beagle rescue groups tend to be even choosier about where they place their Beagles than shelters are. These people are devoted to Beagles and helping the cause of Beagle rescue, so they want to be *very sure* their rescued dogs are going to good, permanent homes. Don't be offended by getting the

FYI: Shelters and Rescue Groups

To find a shelter or rescue group near you, check out these helpful Internet resources:

- **Adopt a Pet Directory** provides a nationwide list of shelters and rescue groups. *www.adoptapet-directory.com*
- **Pet Finder** matches requested breeds to your zip code, providing a complete list of available Beagles near you. Results typically include Beagles and Beagle mixes. *www.petfinder.com*
- **Pets 911.** Enter your zip code and the breed you are searching for and you'll get a list of Beagles and Beagle mixes. *www.pets911.com*
- **Beagle-specific rescue groups** can be found on the National Beagle Club web site. *http://clubs.akc.org/NBC/beagle_rescue.htm*
- **The Beagle Rescue Foundation of America** has compiled a list of Beagle-specific rescue groups around the country. *http://brfoa.tripod.com*

third degree about your home, your life, and your commitment to Beagles. It's all in the best interest of the breed.

Some rarer breeds don't have many dogs in rescue. Not so with Beagles. Thousands of Beagles are relinquished every year because people couldn't handle them. These dogs just want homes where they are loved and understood. You can almost certainly find a purebred Beagle that needs a new home, somewhere near you. Check the sidebar above for Beagle-specific rescue groups that can help you find the right secondhand Beagle for you.

Strays

If you find a stray Beagle or if a stray Beagle comes to your door begging for food, keep in mind that these dogs are clever escape artists and confirmed wanderers. Chances are that Beagle headed out to see what was over the horizon, but has a perfectly good home and worried family looking for him. Do your best to find his original owners: check with the shelter, put up posters, ask around the neighborhood.

If the Beagle has no identification tags or collar, you've checked with the local shelter and veterinarian to be sure he doesn't have a microchip identifying him, and he looks like he's been "out there" for awhile, he might really be a stray needing a new home. Maybe he's just the right dog for you. If you've done your best to be sure he doesn't belong somewhere else, then go ahead. Give him the home he's dreaming of having.

If you really can't keep him (maybe he chases your cat or has a health or temperament problem you can't deal with), consider calling a Beagle rescue group instead of the animal shelter, especially if your shelter euthanizes pets they can't place. Some rescue groups require the dog to go through the shelter process first, but if they know a Beagle is there, they will scoop him up after he is processed through the system. A rescue group will work hard to place the dog in a good home that will appreciate a Beagle for what he really is. Contact the National Beagle Club rescue coordinator for help (*http://clubs.akc.org/NBC/beagle_rescue.htm*)

Papers

Whether you buy or adopt a Beagle, there will be paperwork involved. This is for everyone's information, and in everyone's best interest—including your new Beagle's. The paperwork you will likely receive should include

Purchase or Adoption Contract This should list not only the purchase price or adoption fee, but also your responsibilities, the seller/adopter's responsibilities, and where each party's liabilities begin and end. In the event any party does not fulfill his/her obligations, the paperwork should state what options and recourse each party has. Protect yourself. The seller/adopter will want to be protected, too.

A Health Guarantee The health guarantee, which may or may not be part of the purchase contract, should state what the seller/adopter guarantees (e.g., replacement of the dog in case of serious genetic disease), and what is not guaranteed (such as health issues related to owner negligence, or not related to breeder/adopter negligence). A health guarantee does not guarantee your Beagle will never suffer from a health problem. It is simply a statement of which situations require breeder reparation, such as helping to pay for treatment, or giving you a new dog.

Health Information This includes vaccination records (if available) and records of any veterinary visits, including any prescribed medication.

Care Information A list of what the dog is currently eating, any medications he is currently taking, grooming information, and anything else the seller or adopter feels is necessary or helpful.

Application for Registration of a Purebred Beagle If you buy a puppy that is eligible for registration with the AKC or UKC, registering actually validates the sale because the registry's records will say the puppy still belongs to the breeder until you register it. Also, dogs can't compete in many AKC- or UKC-sponsored events without being registered. To register your dog, you fill out the paperwork (the AKC also allows you to register your dog online) and send in the nominal fee. In a few weeks, you will get your dog's official papers verifying his purebred status and official registration, with whatever name you decide to give him.

FYI: What's in a Pedigree?

Pedigrees can sometimes seem riddled with strange acronyms. Here are some of the most common abbreviations:

- CH: AKC Champion
- CAN.CH: Canadian Champion
- INT.CH: International Champion
- OTCH: Obedience Trial Champion
- BIS: Best in Show winner at an all-breed show
- BISS: Best in Specialty winner at a Beagle specialty show
- FC: Field Champion
- FTC: Canadian Field Trial Champion
- IFC: International Field Champion
- CHB: Certified Hunting Beagle
- CD: Companion Dog (the basic competitive obedience title)
- CDX: Companion Dog Excellent (the next level of competitive obedience title)
- UD: Utility Dog (the third level of competitive obedience title)
- TD: Tracking Dog
- TDX: Tracking Dog Excellent
- TT: Temperament Tested
- CGC: Canine Good Citizen
- AOM: Award of Merit
- LPH: Large Pack on Hare
- SPO: Small Pack Option

Pedigree In the case of a purebred Beagle, when this is available, a breeder should give you a pedigree. A pedigree is a record of the dog's direct descendents. A certified pedigree should include the dog's registration number, registration numbers of the parents (the sire and dam), DNA profile numbers, health registry numbers if applicable (for instance, if the breeder tests the parents of the litter for hip dysplasia or eye disease), stud book numbers, and any "Champion" titles, indicated by "CH" in front of the dog's name. Well-bred Beagle pups from serious hobby breeders should have at least a few champions in the first few generations of the pedigree. Non-certified pedigrees created by the breeder may have additional information, such as "Canine Good Citizen" titles and titles for achievement in certain sports like tracking or hunt tests.

When everything is finally in order, you've chosen your Beagle puppy or rescued adult, and you've signed on the dotted line, you are finally ready to bring your Beagle home with you. Now, the real challenges begin! Keep reading, and you'll know exactly what to expect in the first few days, months, and throughout the life of your soon-to-be-beloved Beagle.

Chapter Four

Caring for a Beagle Puppy

Y ou're finally bringing your Beagle puppy home. Are you sure you are ready? Before your new family member enters the house, you should have already purchased the necessary supplies, made an appointment with your veterinarian, and puppy-proofed your home. After you bring your puppy home, you'll have a lot to do, too. You've got to introduce your new Beagle to the family, show him around, and immediately begin some basic training, such as teaching your Beagle where his personal bathroom is located and where he is supposed to sleep.

You can do it! Just read through this chapter, check off the checklists, and you'll have all your bases covered. Let's start with puppy-proofing.

Puppy-proofing

Snoopy doesn't seem to mind hanging out on the roof of his dog house, but he isn't a new puppy. Your Beagle puppy wants to live inside with you.

But first, you have to make sure his living environment is safe. Puppies, like human babies, are curious and love to test out the world, often with their mouths. Unlike human babies, puppies can move fast, climb high, and chew destructively. They need to be protected from danger, including choking hazards, poisons, and falling objects. Your belongings and furniture need protection, too.

Look around your home and think like a puppy. For a Beagle's-eye point of view, get down on your belly and look around. Where could a puppy go? What could he get into, eat, pull down, or get stuck inside? When you've gotten the lay of the land, stand back up and start puppy proofing. Your efforts should include the following:

- Pick up all small objects off the floor: rubber bands, paper clips, bits of string, stray hair bands, bobby pins, safety pins, backs of earrings, tags from clothing—anything that could pose a choking or poisoning hazard, or that could potentially cause internal injury.

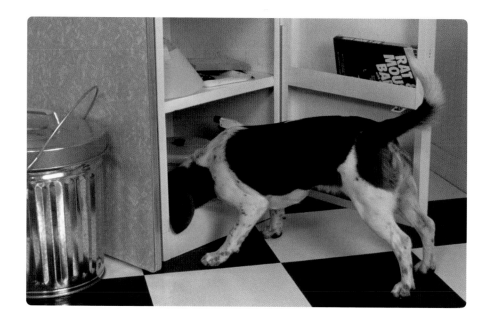

- If it smells good, your Beagle puppy will find it. Put trash inside a cabinet or get a trash can with a secure top. Put all food out of reach, and move cleaning products, pesticides (ant bait, mouse poison), medications, cosmetics, toiletries, and other hazardous and potentially odorous substances behind locked doors or far above puppy-level.
- Certain foods and drinks are particularly poisonous to dogs, including alcohol, coffee, tea, chocolate, onions, grapes, and raisins. Don't leave these or any other foods sitting around within reach of a curious and hungry puppy. Scented candles, air fresheners, and potpourri can also be toxic. Get rid of them or put them up high. Never leave a lighted candle anywhere that a puppy could possibly reach.
- Put baby gates up to block off areas where you don't want your puppy to go, including stairs. New puppies usually do best if they are confined to one or two rooms until they get adjusted to the new home, so choose an area that can take the occasional housetraining accident.
- Block or tape down electrical cords, phone cords, cables, and wires so your puppy doesn't chew them. He could ruin an expensive piece of equipment, or even get an electric shock.
- Block access to any electronic machines that could injure a puppy or that a puppy could destroy, such as paper shredders, computers, and printers.
- Puppies love to chew paper so remove all magazines, "floor files" of important work papers, mail, and newspapers out of reach.
- Tie up any long curtains, mini blind cords, and curtain tassels. Anything dangling may tempt a puppy and could potentially pose a strangulation hazard.

- Do you want to lose your keys? The remote control to the TV? That DVD you just rented? No? Then put them out of reach, too.
- Could your Beagle's happy wagging tail knock it over and break it? Then move it.

Puppy-proofing applies to the garage and the yard, too. Be sure your fence doesn't have any spaces or holes that a puppy could squeeze through, because if anything interesting happens on the other side of the fence, your Beagle will find a way to get out. Some spaces may be too small for an adult Beagle to squeeze through, but not too small for a puppy. These may only need to be blocked temporarily.

Check your garage and driveway for sharp garden tools, lawn chemicals, and other hazards. Anti-freeze spills on the floor or driveway pose a serious threat—just a few licks of the sweet-tasting liquid can quickly spell death to a dog, so make sure you don't have any leaks.

CAUTION

Lawn chemicals are hazardous to puppies, so look into organic lawn care options before bringing home your puppy. Many outdoor bushes, plants, and flowers including lilies, sago palm, tulip and daffodil bulbs, azaleas, rhododendron, oleander, chrysanthemum, and English ivy are also poisonous to dogs. It is best to remove these from the property or block access to them. For a complete list of outdoor and indoor plants that could be toxic to pets, check out the ASPCA Poison Control Center Web site at *www.aspca.org/apcc.* Click on "Toxic Plants."

Puppy Supplies

Your house is safe, but is it well-supplied? To tell the truth, puppies don't need as much stuff as some pet supply stores would like you to think, but you will need some supplies to keep your puppy healthy and safe.

Must-have Basics

You can skip the fancy dog bed, the argyle dog sweater, and the toy-for-every-day-of-the-year. You can even skip the gourmet dog treats, although your Beagle might beg (literally) to differ. There are, however, some items you and your Beagle can't do without.

Crate or Kennel Dogs are den animals and they get very attached to their own personal space, especially if it is safely enclosed like a den. A plastic crate or kennel draped with a blanket over the top, sides, and back, will make your pup feel very safe and makes a great place for a time-out when life gets too hectic to have a Beagle underfoot. Your Beagle will soon seek out this space when he needs some down-time. The crate or kennel will also become an indispensable tool when you housetrain your Beagle puppy and will keep him safe when you can't supervise him.

Choose a crate just big enough for your Beagle to stand up, turn around, lie down, and stretch out. If the crate is big enough that your Beagle puppy

can sleep on one side and use the other side for a bathroom, it is too big and won't be a useful housetraining aid.

Soft Bedding for Crate or Kennel You weren't going to let your Beagle puppy lie on that hard plastic or wire grate, were you? Perish the thought. You can buy cushioned, plush pads that fit inside the crate or kennel you choose, but an appropriately-sized flat pillow or a soft, folded blanket or towel will do just as well.

Pet Seatbelt Unless you purchase a crate or kennel that straps safely into your backseat, you will need some way to keep your Beagle safe in the car. Pet seatbelts attach your Beagle's harness to the car's regular seatbelt so that your Beagle won't get thrown around. Pet seatbelts reduce the likelihood of injury to both pets and people in the event of an accident.

Breed Needs

Did you buckle up your Beagle on the way home? Every time you ride in the car with a dog, you should both be safely secured in case of an accident. Unsecured dogs can not only escape after an accident when they are scared and possibly injured, but can seriously injure other passengers. Fortunately, you can buy many different kinds of dog seatbelts, or crates that buckle into the car. Don't leave home without one! I particularly like the Ruff Rider canine auto restrain system (*www.ruffrider.com*) and the Kurgo Auto Zip Line (*www.kurgo.com*).

SHOPPING LIST

New Puppy Supplies

Make a copy of this abbreviated shopping list and take it to the pet store with you so you don't forget anything you need for your new Beagle puppy.

- Crate or kennel for housetraining and safety
- Soft bedding for the crate or kennel
- Pet seatbelt
- Collar with ID tags
- Leash
- High-quality puppy food
- Metal or ceramic food and water bowls
- Soft, natural bristle brush for puppies
- Hound mitt and/or rubber curry comb for adults
- Nail trimmer for small-to-medium dogs
- Gentle dog shampoo

- Toothbrush and toothpaste made for dogs
- Safe chew toys
- Stain and odor-removing spray for housetraining accidents

Optional
- Dog bed
- More chew toys
- Fetching toys
- Tug toys
- "Smart toys"
- Healthy treats
- Extra collars and leashes
- Pet gates
- Outdoor dog house
- Dog travel gear
- Dog clothes and accessories
- Eco-friendly pet products

Collar with I.D. Tags For wander-lusting Beagles, identification tags are very important. If your puppy ever escapes, tags will make it much easier for anyone who finds him to contact you and return him. Your puppy also needs a soft, comfortable nylon collar. Look for adjustable collars that can grow with your puppy. Once your Beagle is full-sized, you can invest in a more permanent nylon, leather, or hemp collar that fits correctly.

Leash Your new puppy won't understand how to walk on a leash, but you will teach him. A short 4-foot leash will be lighter and easier to use on a small puppy. When he's grown, you'll want a 6-foot leash, or a retractable leash that will allow your Beagle to explore, but still stay safely under your control.

High-quality Puppy Food Talk to the breeder and/or your veterinarian about the best food for your puppy, and don't skimp. Cheap food isn't worth the bargain price because it often results in much more waste, and possibly even a less healthy puppy. For more on how to pick a good dog food, see Chapter 6.

Metal or Ceramic Food and Water Bowls Beagles can chew up a plastic bowl, and plastic harbors bacteria. Metal and ceramic are easy to disinfect in the dishwasher and your Beagle won't be able to dismantle them with his mouth.

Natural Bristle Brush for Puppies Get your Beagle puppy in the habit of sitting nicely for grooming, and he'll enjoy this time together as he grows older. Beagles don't need complicated grooming tools. A soft, natural bristle brush is perfect for a puppy.

Hound Mitt or Rubber Curry Comb for Adult Beagles As your Beagle gets older and starts shedding more, try a hound mitt or a rubber curry comb. These tools effectively remove shedding hair, but because they aren't as soft as a natural bristle brush, they are better for adult Beagles who are a little larger and more accustomed to grooming.

Nail Trimmer for Small-to-Medium Dogs Beagles are good at digging, and have the strong nails to prove it. That doesn't mean they like getting their nails clipped, however. Start puppies early to get them used to nail clipping by clipping just the tiny tips about once a week. (For more on how to clip your Beagle's nails, see Chapter 8.)

Gentle Dog Shampoo Some Beagles have sensitive skin, so look for a shampoo specifically formulated for dogs (not for people) that is gentle, hypo-allergenic, and preferably contains no sudsing agents that can irritate skin. Organic and natural formulas are usually more gentle and often contain botanical ingredients to soothe, heal, and strengthen skin. (For more on shampooing your Beagle, see Chapter 8.)

Toothbrush and Toothpaste Made for Dogs Get your puppy used to brushing at a young age and make it a lifelong habit to head off tooth decay as your Beagle gets older. Veterinary dentists say brushing every day, or at least once a week, is one of the best things you can do for your dog's health. (For more on how to brush your dog's teeth and why it's so important, see Chapter 8.)

Breed Needs

Hound mitts and rubber curry combs reduce shedding by efficiently removing dead hair from a hound coat. They also stimulate the skin to produce healthy coat oils, and even increase circulation. A hound mitt fits over your hand like a glove and has little rubber nubs on the palm. Just "pet" your Beagle, rubbing the nubs all over his coat. A rubber curry comb is a hard rubber grooming tool that looks a little like a scrub brush, but with rubber nubs instead of bristles.

Safe Chew Toys Beagle puppies need to chew, and they need safe ways to do it. If a Beagle puppy always has a satisfying chew toy near, he won't have to resort to your shoes, the legs of the sofa, or the kids' toys. Choose durable chew toys without small pieces that could break off and cause choking. Toys, including rope toys, made of hemp are safer than some other fabrics because hemp is actually digestible. Companies I like: The Good Dog (*www.thegooddogcompany.com*) and Earth Dog (*www.earthdog.com*). Also, check out Silly Kitty which, despite the name, sells rope chews for dogs (*www.sillykitty.ca*).

Stain and Odor-removing Spray for Housetraining Accidents Vigilance will minimize accidents in the house, but we all slip up sometimes and miss the signs that our puppies need to go outside. When that happens, don't give your Beagle puppy the chance to smell a past accident and mistakenly think it's okay to "go" there again. Clean it up stat with a cleaner that obliterates, rather than masks, odor. Look for varieties containing enzymes.

Helpful Hints

Love your Beagle and the earth, too? It's now easier than ever to be both well-supplied and eco-friendly, thanks to the hundreds of pet products now available that are natural, organic, recyclable, and sustainably produced. Look for organic pet food and treats, leashes and collars made from hemp, organic and natural botanical grooming products, pet beds made from organic cotton and stuffed with recycled material, and pet toys made from recycled, recyclable, natural, organic, and other "green" materials.

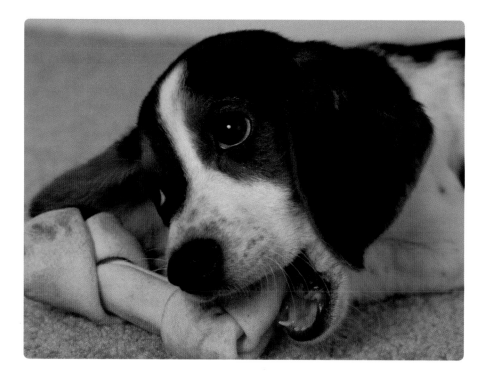

Optional Fun Stuff If you've got some extra cash and you want to spoil your Beagle puppy just a little, then why not? A wider selection of chew toys and other play toys for fetching and tug, complete with a doggy toy box, can be fun. Some toys are specially designed to challenge a dog's mental capacity. These so-called "smart toys" require dogs to unpuzzle them to get to a treat or other reward. Healthy gourmet treats are always welcome, too. Some Beagles won't sleep in a dog bed, preferring their crates or kennels, or even a cozy spot in bed with you, but others love their dog beds, and dog beds come in a huge array of fashionable styles, from inexpensive to high-end. Browse the pet store shelves and you're sure to find other tempting items: fancier dog collars and matching leashes, posh dog houses for outdoor time, telescoping pet gates to fit any entrance, pet travel accessories such as portable bowls and quilted strap-on seat covers for the car, even doggy coats, boots, hats, and sunglasses.

The First Day

The first few days with a new puppy can be extra challenging, not unlike the first few days with a new baby. Your Beagle doesn't know where he's going or where he has arrived. Your home, so familiar to you, is foreign territory to him. He doesn't yet know your rules or what is normal in your home. He'll learn all these things quickly (Beagles are smart), but you can help ease the transition.

How you handle the first few days can make a huge difference in how quickly your Beagle adjusts. Remember that your new Beagle needs to know five important things:

- Where his bathroom is located.
- Where he will rest and sleep.
- Where he will eat.
- Who else lives in the house, including other people and animals.
- That he is safe and secure with you in charge.

Communicating the answers to these important issues isn't that hard if you minimize your Beagle's stress and commotion and keep the first day relatively calm, quiet, and low-key. Don't expect too much from your new pup at first. He will be under stress, and needs some time to get used to you and figure out some things for himself. You can help.

Breed Needs

Most breeders, animal shelters, and rescue groups require a check-up from a veterinarian within the first day or two after bringing home a new puppy. Often, a documented veterinarian visit is required to activate the health guarantee. A veterinarian should always see a new puppy to check for any minor health problems, signs of serious disease, and to get a baseline of health for the puppy, in order to measure future growth and changes. Don't neglect this important visit! If possible, take your puppy to the veterinarian on the way home from the breeder. At the very least, your puppy should see your veterinarian for a check-up within the first 48 hours after bringing him home.

Give Your Beagle a Bathroom Break

When you first arrive home with your new Beagle, don't take him inside yet. First, take him to the place you want him to use as a bathroom. Puppies need to piddle frequently, and although your Beagle might be too busy sniffing around, give him a chance to use the spot, just in case he needs it after the drive home.

When you take him to this spot, keep him on his leash, even if you have a fenced yard. In the early weeks, your Beagle should learn to do his business while on the leash. Then, as a reward, he gets to run around without the leash for awhile, checking out all the interesting new smells in your yard. Go to the spot and stop. Watch him but don't talk to him and don't make it obvious that you are watching. If he piddles, praise him gently and warmly, then let him off the leash. If he just sits there, waiting for you to do something, wait him out for at least five minutes. If he really doesn't need to go, let him explore the yard, still on leash. Keep watching. If he eventually decides to do his thing, praise him. If he's really not going to do it, then it's time to take him inside for a short while. Return to the yard in 15 or 20 minutes, though. You want him to ace his first housetraining lesson. (For more on housetraining, see Chapter 5.)

Show Your Beagle Around

After you've explored the yard, it's time to go inside. For now, put other pets away. Your Beagle needs a chance to get his bearings, without the stress of another dog or cat trying to tell him who's boss. If you have children, ask them to stand back for a few minutes. They can watch, but should remain calm and keep their voices down. No mobbing the puppy!

Show your Beagle the places that he will be allowed to go. If you've gated a certain room or two, let him explore. Show him his food and water bowl (very important to your Beagle!). Show him his crate, but don't put him in it just yet. Let him sniff around. If you toss a few treats inside, he may go in there on his own. If he doesn't, don't worry. Remember, you want to keep the mood relaxed and happy.

If you let your Beagle puppy explore on his own, he'll gain confidence and get to know his new home more quickly than if you never let his feet touch the floor or surround him with cooing, ooh-ing, and ahh-ing family members.

After your Beagle has had a good sniff session, and maybe a little snack and some water, take him back outside to his special spot, on his leash, and give him another chance to do his business. Then, it's back inside to meet the family.

Meeting the Family

Yes, I know, the kids have been chomping at the bit. They can hardly stand it. They want to hold the new puppy. Of course they do! What could be cuter than a tiny Beagle pup? However, kids need a serious lesson in dog handling before they are allowed to play with the puppy. Make sure your children understand the following rules:

- Do not carry the puppy around. Only play with the puppy while sitting on the floor. A puppy that gets dropped or jumps out of a child's arms could get seriously injured. Beagles are sturdier than some breeds, but all puppies are fragile and your puppy could break a leg if he gets dropped or if a wobbly toddler falls on him.
- Do not swamp the puppy with too much attention. Puppies can get scared if they are over-stimulated. Kids should take turns, stay calm, and keep their voices down. Puppies need to feel like the humans in the house are in charge and they don't have to worry or be afraid. That includes kids. There will be plenty of time, as the puppy grows, for loud and boisterous play out in the yard. The first day is not that time.
- Don't let the puppy chew on fingers! Puppies need to learn that dog teeth should not touch human skin. Instruct your kids (and other family members and friends) to offer chew toys, not fingers, for puppy teeth. If the puppy does try to chew on fingers, clothes, or anything else off limits, say "No!" sharply, and pull away. Then, offer an acceptable chew toy and praise the puppy when he chews the right thing.

Introducing Other Pets

If you have other dogs or cats, birds, even small animals, your Beagle should meet them. However, it is your job to make sure the interaction remains positive and friendly. If you have a gentle, friendly dog or cat, take him out and let him sniff the puppy, and vice versa. See how they interact. At the first sign of any discomfort, anxiety, or aggression, remove the puppy to a separate room.

If you think your resident pet may have a problem with a new puppy at first, your introduction can be more gradual. After the puppy has spent some time in a room in your home, take him to a different room and close the door. (Someone should stay in there with him to keep an eye on him.)

Helpful Hints

When you bring home a new Beagle puppy, your resident pet will probably feel slighted and a little jealous for awhile. He may act angry with you, or ignore you. This is normal, and the solution is to lavish your older pet with attention. Even though it is exciting to have such an adorable puppy in the house, your previous pet has been with you for a long time and needs to know he is not being replaced. Take extra time alone with him and don't make it all about the puppy.

Then let your resident pet come in and sniff around, so he smells the presence of another dog before seeing the dog. If your dog pees where he smells the puppy, even if he would never normally pee in the house, that's a sign that he's marking his territory. He wants the puppy to know he is in charge. Be patient.

Switch your two pets back and forth between rooms, even for a few days, so each gets plenty of opportunities to smell the other. You can even let them sniff and bark and paw at each other under a door or on either side of a baby gate. Once each pet seems accustomed to the other's presence, you can let them interact, but stay in control of the situation. Enlist help if necessary.

In many cases, the resident pet won't like the new puppy at first, especially if the puppy constantly pesters the other pet to play. You may be disappointed that they aren't immediately friends, but this is completely normal. Just give them both time, stay in charge of the situation, and never let interactions progress to the point of a fight. Also, give your resident pet lots of attention and reassurance, so she doesn't feel threatened or jealous. Be especially careful if you have a dog that is much larger than your Beagle puppy, or a cat that has front claws. Reward all civil behavior with mutual treats and lots of attention. In most cases, with good supervision, resident pets will accept and even befriend a Beagle puppy. In a few months, they may be inseparable.

Introducing the Crate or Kennel

After all the excitement of a new home, new smells, new people, and new animals, your Beagle puppy is probably feeling a little overwhelmed. Even if

he still acts excited, he may be overstimulated. To minimize stress, he needs some down time.

Take him outside to the yard for one more potty break, on the leash. If he takes one, great. Praise him. If not, that's fine, too. Just give him the chance. Now, it's time to introduce him to his crate or kennel—Your Beagle puppy's home within a home, his Beagle Bungalow.

This special place will soon become a place of quiet refuge for your Beagle, and an invaluable housetraining aid. Crates also make it easy to transport your Beagle, whether to the veterinarian, or in case of emergency. In a strange place, the crate will serve as a familiar and comforting safe place for your Beagle, but he doesn't know that yet. Take your Beagle to his crate and throw in a treat. If he goes inside, great. If not, gently place him inside. Close the door, reassure him, then go about your business. If you are using a wire kennel, be sure to drape a blanket over the top, sides, and back, so your Beagle feels safely enclosed.

Your puppy may whine, cry, howl, or make any number of Beagle-esque noises. That's fine. It might be difficult, but ignore him. He needs to learn that nothing bad happens when he is in the crate. Stay in sight but don't act agitated. Offer the occasional comforting noise but don't make a fuss. This is an important lesson for your puppy, and although he may sound like he is dying in there, he is not. He's just whining because he doesn't know what's going on. This is how he learns.

If he settles down and decides to take a nap, great. If he keeps whining, let him carry on for about 15 minutes. Then, during a lull in the whining (if there is one), say, "Okay, time to come out!" (or something similar) in a cheerful voice. Don't offer coddling and sympathy. Take him out, put on his leash, and take him straight out to the backyard to his special spot. Puppies often need to piddle after a rest. Give him the opportunity.

For the rest of the day, alternate between playing with and watching your Beagle puppy, and letting him rest in his crate when you can't watch him closely. Leaving him alone for short periods teaches independence, so he doesn't become too needy, but new puppies shouldn't stay in their crates for more than two hours at a time. This won't last for too long—soon he'll be able to stay in there a little longer. But for now, gradually work up to two hour rest periods over the next few days.

Before long, your Beagle will look forward to his crate time. It may take a few days, even a week or two, but when you can't watch him, his crate is the safest place for him to be. Remember, puppies need a lot of play time, a lot of potty breaks, and a lot of rest. Dogs are den animals by nature and have an instinct to seek out enclosed spaces. Balance out his day appropriately and he'll soon come to trust and rely on you to give him exactly what he needs.

The First Night

Fun Facts

If you think your Beagle puppy is making a lot of noise when you first put him in his crate, just wait until the first night. Most puppies cry, whine, and howl in protest when you put them in their crates at night. It's no wonder. Your puppy is used to being with his mother and littermates. Now, he's all alone in the dark in a strange place.

According to the National Sleep Foundation's 2008 survey, 14 percent of women surveyed allow pets to share their beds, and these are among the women experiencing the most sleep disturbances.

It's easy to take pity on your pup and bring him into bed with you, but this isn't a great idea until he's housetrained, and maybe not even then, unless you don't mind Beagle hair on your pillow. If you let him cry it out, you'll be rewarded with quiet after a few nights. Or not! Some Beagles never adjust to a crate and are much happier in a dog bed beside you. It all depends on your puppy, and your individual tolerance for the situation.

But here's the great thing about Beagles: They are independent. They aren't a needy breed constantly looking for attention and coddling. If you teach your Beagle puppy to sleep nicely in his crate now, you will be supporting his natural independence.

If you do choose to let him sleep in a dog bed or in bed with you, that's fine, too. Just remember that he will probably need a bathroom break in the middle of the night. Young puppies can't go an entire night without a bathroom break, but those in a crate will usually doze off, then wake up and whine to tell you they are ready to go out. If he's not confined, he may not wake you up to tell you about it. He may just go off and take care of his needs on your carpet . . . or on your pillow.

After the first few weeks, your puppy will probably be able to go all night without a bathroom break, and will likely go to sleep inside his little den without any fuss at all. He may even start going to bed on his own when he gets tired. Congratulations! You'll start getting more sleep, and life will take on a new, regular rhythm that both you and your Beagle can depend upon.

Helpful Hints

If you are still having problems at night after your puppy is three months old, talk to your veterinarian to rule out a health problem, then ask a good dog obedience instructor for advice. By then, your Beagle should be registered in a puppy training class, so you will have more guidance. Someone who can look at your individual situation and puppy and see what you are doing right and wrong should be able to offer customized advice to help you.

Chapter Five

Living with a Beagle

As you settle in with your Beagle and get to know each other, life is going to be a little bit different than it was before. You're living with a Beagle now. You've got to contend with those strange Beagle noises, significant puppy needs, and all that energy!

You've also got to spend the next couple of years instilling some important knowledge into your Beagle. From housetraining in the early weeks to socialization throughout your Beagle's life, you've got a lot to think about. Of course, your rewards will be ample, as you and your Beagle develop a relationship and sense of camaraderie, but that won't happen overnight, or without a little bit of effort. This chapter is here to help.

Housetraining

For many puppy owners, housetraining is the first thing on the puppy to-do list. After all, your living room carpet is not a bathroom, is it? If you want to keep your house clean and sanitary and your Beagle well-mannered and under control, you have to contend with housetraining, starting on the very first day you bring your Beagle home.

Fortunately, most Beagles learn pretty quickly, as long as you are willing to instruct them. Beagles are smart and they don't want to make you angry. Ignore the situation, however, and you can't expect your Beagle to know what you want. Beagles do the best they can with the knowledge they have.

The best way to give your Beagle the knowledge he needs is through a combination of crate training and schedule training.

Crate Training

Crate training is a popular and effective method of housetraining in which the puppy stays in the crate whenever you can't watch him, but never for longer than he can go without having an accident. The theory is that dogs don't like to soil their dens, so they won't have accidents while inside the crate. If the crate is the proper size—just big enough for your puppy to stand up, turn around, and stretch out, but not so big that he can sleep on

HOME BASICS
It's OK to Crate

Some people think crate training is cruel, but when done correctly it's kind. Dogs like being safe in their dens, and they like to please you. Crate training teaches them how to behave appropriately and when coupled with lots of praise and rewards, results in a very happy Beagle. Crate training only becomes cruel if you leave your puppy inside a crate for too long—more than two hours for a very young puppy, and more than four hours for an older puppy of 16 weeks or more. Young puppies can't hold their urine for longer than two hours, and because Beagles are active dogs, even adults shouldn't have to sit in a crate for more than four hours.

one side and use the other side as a bathroom—he probably won't soil his crate unless you leave him in there for too long.

Whenever you take your puppy out of the crate, you take him immediately to his place in the yard, on a leash, and wait until he does his business. Spend some time playing, and when you can't watch him anymore, it's back in the crate.

Use the crate correctly and your Beagle will become housetrained quickly. After a couple of weeks of crate training, most Beagles have it all figured out—where to go, and where not to go. Many people continue to use the

crate when their Beagles need to be confined for any reason, for travel, and for a dog bed. Others graduate from the crate and rarely go back inside.

Every now and then, a puppy breaks the rules and does have accidents in his crate, even when the crate is not overly large and you aren't leaving the puppy inside for too long. Chances are, you are to blame. Did you ignore his pleading glances or wait too long to let him out? Sometimes, accidents are a symptom of a health problem, so check with your veterinarian. If everything checks out, consider schedule training instead, or a combination of the two methods. A good obedience instructor may also be able to help you sort out the issue.

Schedule Training

Schedule training is a method in which you take the puppy out at exactly the same times every day, so he always has a chance to do his business in the appropriate area. As always, take him out on a leash, to his spot, and wait for him to go. When he does, praise him and let him off the leash for some playtime in the yard.

You have to be organized and vigilant to be a good schedule trainer if you don't also use the crate, because if you miss a scheduled pit stop, your Beagle will probably just find a good place in the house and piddle there instead of waiting for you to notice he has to go. But when practiced diligently, schedule training works, and it's a great option for dogs or people who really object to the crate.

Helpful Hints

Many people prefer to use a combination of housetraining and schedule training. They always take their puppies out on a strict schedule, according to the puppy's age and needs, but when they can't watch the puppy, they keep him in his crate for safety and to help prevent accidents. This method is very effective, as long as you stick to the schedule and always keep an eye on the puppy when he isn't in his crate.

To make schedule training efficient, it helps to know something about puppies. Young puppies, from about 8 to 16 weeks, need to go out about every two hours during the day, and about every four hours during the night. Puppies also tend to need a bathroom break every time they have

- Recently eaten
- Played vigorously
- Just gotten up from a nap

If you forget and your puppy has an accident in the house, his progress will backtrack and he may begin to think it's okay to use the carpet for a bathroom after all. Watch your puppy closely for signs he needs to go, such as sniffing and walking in circles. If he starts to squat, scoop him up quickly and rush him outside. Clean up any mess with an odor-dissolving cleaner as soon as you find it and don't scold the puppy (he won't know why you are scolding him).

Schedule training can take longer than crate training because of the greater possibility for accidents and because it may take awhile to get to know your puppy's individual schedule. Some puppies simply have to go out more often than others. But once you figure out your puppy's tendencies and always take him out on schedule, he'll learn that the bathroom is located *outside.*

Puppy Grooming

Your tiny little puppy hardly sheds at all, and his little nails don't look very long. You don't really have to start grooming him right away, do you? Actually, if you begin grooming at least once a week when your Beagle puppy is very young, he will get used to the process and be a much better customer as he gets older and needs more frequent brushing and nail clipping.

Unlike some dogs with longer coats, Beagles don't need a lot of upkeep. Still, many don't like having their nails clipped and may wonder what the heck you are doing with that bristly business all over their backs. Grooming now teaches your Beagle puppy what is expected of him later. It also gets him used to handling, so that when a veterinarian needs to look at his paws or peek inside his ears or examine his teeth, he won't be confused or nervous.

Grooming never has to take a lot of time, and for a Beagle puppy, it is truly quick and easy. About once a week, or even daily if you have the time, do the following:

1. Give your puppy a brief rubdown to loosen shed hair and stimulate circulation.
2. Check his paw pads, his teeth, under his tail, and his belly, feeling for lumps, and looking for tooth or gum issues like swollen areas or decay.

CHECKLIST

Puppy Grooming Supplies

Keep these supplies handy for puppy grooming sessions:

✔ Soft bristle brush
✔ Nail clipper made for dogs

✔ Cotton balls
✔ Soft toothbrush
✔ Toothpaste made for dogs
✔ Small healthy treats

This will be a huge help to your veterinarian. As your Beagle ages, this is also a very important practice that could help you to catch a health problem before it gets too advanced.

3. Brush your puppy's coat with a soft bristle brush, lightly and gently. Praise him as you go.
4. With a nail clipper made for dogs, clip off just the very tips of his nails about once a week, or as often as necessary. If he doesn't need his nails clipped, touch the clipper to each nail, just to get him used to the process.
5. Wash out the parts of his ears you can see with a wet cotton ball, to get him used to ear handling and cleaning.
6. With a soft brush and a tiny dab of toothpaste made for dogs, brush your Beagle's teeth. Get him used to this now and enjoy good dental health (and much lower veterinarian bills) later in your Beagle's life.
7. Give him a treat! If he learns that grooming ends with a treat, he may start bringing the brush to *you*.

Socialization

In case you forgot, your Beagle is not a human. He's a dog. In other words, his natural instinct is to do doggy things, including things that don't always work out so well when living with fussy humans. To learn how to live peacefully and successfully in a human world, a Beagle needs socialization.

Socialization is the process of introducing your Beagle to the social elements of human life. This includes meeting a lot of different kinds of people—tall, short, older, younger, babies, toddlers, people in wheelchairs, people with hats, people with beards, people of all shapes and sizes and colors.

Socialization also means meeting a lot of different animals—other dogs of all sizes, cats, birds. And socialization means encountering all kinds of different places and situations: neighborhoods, busy traffic areas, hiking trails, other people's yards, the insides of cars, the veterinarian's office, the pet store, the baseball or soccer field, the drive-through, the dog park.

Socializing your Beagle puppy is easy, but comes with an important rule. Take your Beagle to lots of different places, but (this is the important part)

always make sure the experience is positive. Puppies that have traumatic experiences with cruel or careless people or aggressive dogs often grow up with fears and even aggressive tendencies that are very hard to fix. If your Beagle learns that the world is friendly, he will grow up to be friendly. If he learns the world is dangerous and unsafe, he won't be such a friendly fellow.

In other words, expose your Beagle to the world, but protect him while you do it. Make sure he gets lots of reinforcement for his naturally outgoing and curious behavior, and doesn't get punished for being a Beagle. Luckily, most people out there in the world have a soft spot in their hearts for the Snoopy dog, so with a little caution, your job should be easy.

Puppy Training Classes

One of the best ways to begin socializing your Beagle puppy is by signing up for a puppy training class, sometimes called puppy kindergarten or puppy socialization class. These classes, led by an instructor, help begin socialization, in addition to teaching some very basic, easy commands such as *sit* and *come*. Fun, light-hearted, and a great place to meet other puppy owners, puppy classes provide the opportunity to start your Beagle off on the right paw. You will typically learn a lot and get exercises for you and your Beagle to practice during at-home training sessions, and you should be able to ask your instructor for help dealing with basic issues at home, including housetraining problems, puppy nipping, and training your Beagle not to be a nuisance.

After your Beagle puppy graduates from puppy class, he should be ready for a basic obedience class, another important part of teaching your Beagle how to behave in a human world. For more on training see Chapter 7.

Establishing a Routine

Adding a Beagle to the household requires a change in lifestyle. However, the most important thing you can do to assure your Beagle feels comfortable, safe, and adjusts quickly, is to create a daily routine and stick with it.

Dogs crave routine, and while some adjust to sudden changes better than others, all do better if they know what to expect. Waking up, meal and nap times, bathroom breaks, walks and training sessions should all be on a schedule. Your Beagle should learn what it means when you grab your purse or your briefcase or lace up your running shoes. Will he be heading to his crate? Coming along? Creating and sticking to a schedule will do your Beagle a big favor. You'll be happier, too, as your Beagle adjusts more quickly and behaves better.

Your routine doesn't have to be rigid, but it should consist of regular meal times (the same number of meals and same general times for meals each day), nap times, outdoor times, walks, training sessions, and grooming. As your Beagle learns to anticipate and expect these regular events, he'll begin to tune in to your schedule. This fosters better communication between you and your Beagle, and you might even find your Beagle listens to you more attentively. Obviously, schedules occasionally get disrupted, but if your Beagle knows what is normal for you and your life, he'll quickly adopt that version of normal for himself.

Help, my Beagle Puppy Is . . .

He's cute. He's cuddly. And sometimes, he's downright frustrating, confusing, annoying, or worrisome. Here's how to handle Beagle behavior.

Biting Puppies naturally explore the world with their mouths, but those tiny teeth are sharp. Puppies must learn *bite inhibition* at a young age, and it's your job to teach them. Every single time puppy teeth touch human skin or clothing, yell "No!" and pull away, then immediately offer your puppy an appropriate chew toy. If he bites that instead, praise him lavishly. Instruct other family members and friends to do the same.

Agressive Behavior Beagles should never be aggressive, so if a puppy is biting aggressively, rather than out of a sense of exploration or play, there is probably something wrong. Either the puppy is being threatened and

Breed Truths

Because Beagles are so intelligent and learn so much through their noses, meeting the world in all its variety teaches them a lot about people, other animals, and situations. They learn what is normal and what is not normal, what you like and what you fear. Beagles aren't natural guardians, but socialization can refine their watchdog skills, and help them react in a healthy way to life in a human world. Despite the way they sometimes behave, Beagles are pretty tuned in to what the people around them are doing and even thinking. Well-socialized Beagles almost always behave better, listen better, and make better decisions with their independent brains.

should not be put in the frightening situation, or the puppy has a medical or serious behavioral problem. Aggression is more common in older dogs who have learned to be aggressive in response to a situation such as abuse or neglect. See your veterinarian to rule out health problems, then seek out help from a certified animal behaviorist who can help you figure out what is going on. Some trainers have experience dealing with aggression, but avoid those who use dominance methods and manhandling, which usually just makes the situation worse. Aggression is a serious problem and must be dealt with immediately. Don't put it off. A normal, healthy Beagle that isn't being seriously threatened or hurt should never be aggressive.

Barking When your Beagle goes on a barking binge, take the puppy inside and distract him with a toy or treat or give him a time-out in his crate, with something satisfying to chew on, until he calms down. Avoid bark-triggering situations by keeping puppy-level windows covered and taking the dog inside during times of heavy neighborhood traffic. That being said, living with a Beagle means accepting a certain amount of noise.

Chewing Beagles should never be given the opportunity to chew on shoes, toys, or furniture. Keep these objects away from the puppy, and always have plenty of appropriate chew toys at hand. If your Beagle starts gnawing on something you don't want him to chew, distract him with a sharp "No!" then offer him a chew toy. Don't forget to praise appropriate chewing whenever possible. For problem areas your Beagle just can't stay away from, consider spraying with a chew-deterrent such as Bitter Apple, which makes furniture, rugs, pillows, etc. taste horrible. If you do use a chew-deterrent spray, follow the package directions.

Crying If your Beagle whines and cries because you put him in his crate, he is learning patience. Let him learn. If, however, he seems to be in pain, or cries after a fall, call your veterinarian immediately. If he whines after being inside his crate for more than an hour, he's probably bored silly or he really needs to go outside. Pay attention and don't ignore your Beagle's needs, and he'll learn that you really are a trustworthy guardian.

Ignoring You Your Beagle is so fascinated with all the exciting and irresistible smells in the world that he can't be expected to pay attention to you every second. Let him be a Beagle and exercise his scenting ability to his

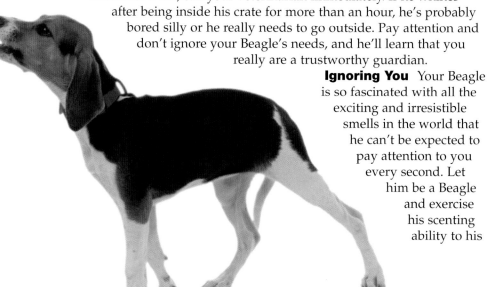

heart's content, and when he's good and ready, he'll come to you for the affection you both crave. If, however, your Beagle puppy acts unusually tired, sluggish, or unresponsive, he may have a medical problem. In this case, call your veterinarian right away.

Escaping Beagles are clever and persistent escape artists. They aren't made for sitting in a yard all day, they are made for running through miles of forests and pasturelands after rabbits. Beagles often escape if they are bored or something more interesting is going on over the fence, so the first thing to do for an escape artist is give him a lot more to do. More exercise, more training, more toys, more activity, more time with you.

Some Beagles will try to escape no matter what you do. Beagles aren't traffic-smart, so for their own safety they must never be allowed to wander free. If you let your Beagle outside, he needs to be on a leash or within a fence, and not just any fence. Be sure yours is high enough that he can't climb out, and buried deep enough in the ground, or otherwise barricaded, so he can't dig under. Block areas where he could squeeze between poles or beneath fencing.

CAUTION

When you are looking for puppy training classes in your area, ask about the training techniques. Some trainers still use harsh old-fashioned methods. Positive reinforcement training works best, *especially* for Beagles, so confirm that the instructor is a proponent of positive reinforcement training. You might even ask if you can sit in on a class and watch, just to get a feel for the instructor's style. If you like it and feel comfortable, sign right up. It could be the best thing you do for your Beagle. Find a positive reinforcement trainer near you through the Association of Pet Dog Trainers (APDT) (*www.apdt.com*).

This might take some effort, but it is extremely important for your Beagle's well-being. Cinderblocks around the bottom of the fence line can be a good temporary solution until you can pour cement or build something more permanent. Remember, Beagles like to dig, so you have to make your fence dig-proof. Building a solid privacy fence can also help because the Beagle can no longer see what is on the other side. This may make him less likely to try to get out. Or, he might just consider it a bigger challenge.

In a very few cases, even the most seemingly secure fences can't keep a Beagle inside. For very serious and dedicated escape artists, you may need to enlist the help of technology. Ask your local pet store or farm store about electric fencing if you simply can't keep your Beagle on your property.

Digging Speaking of digging, did I mention Beagles enjoy it? Not every Beagle has the urge to resurface your backyard, but some of them think it's pretty darned fun. Rather than fight it, why not give your Beagle a place to dig? Some people put in small sand boxes for their dogs because sand makes less of a mess than dirt. To tempt your Beagle, hide small treats in the sand, and encourage your Beagle to dig them out. He'll soon forget all about digging up your tulip bulbs. If you don't want to put a sandbox in your yard—there are downsides, such as attracting cats to use the box as a giant bathroom—remember that Beagles sometimes dig out of boredom. Give your Beagle more exercise and more to do besides digging up the yard.

Just too Active! Young Beagles are active. If they sit at home alone all day waiting for you to come home, of course they will go a little crazy when you get home. They want to move, run, play! They want to *be Beagles.* Tired or not, if you have taken on the responsibility of a young Beagle, you need to take him out and get him some good hard exercise. Every day. Or, if that just doesn't work for you, consider another excellent option for Beagles: Doggy Daycare.

Doggy Daycare: The Perfect Solution for Active Beagles

You might be exhausted from your day at work. Maybe all you want to do is relax. Guess what? There *is* a perfect solution. One that is increasingly available to working dog owners all over the country. *Doggy daycare.* Yes, you heard right. Daycare for dogs is just like daycare for kids. You drop off your dog in the morning and pick him up after work. In the meantime, he gets to spend the day running around inside and out, playing with other dogs, having snacks, and generally amusing and (here's the key) *exhausting* himself. While some breeds that tend to be scrappy with other dogs don't always do well in daycare, friendly and sociable Beagles tend to love it. When you get home after your long day at work, he is also getting home from his long day at play, and he'll be much more likely to chill out and watch television with you. A nice leisurely walk around the block is fine for Beagles who are also getting a lot of exercise in daycare.

And the cost? It depends on where you live and how much competition there is, but many people say the cost is more than well worth the benefits, which include a better socialized, better exercised, and more well adjusted Beagle. However, check out doggy daycare facilities carefully. The facility should be clean and have a lot of space for dogs to play. Make sure the people who are in charge of the dogs are well trained and know how to deal with any conflicts that might develop between dogs. Ask about their training and experience. The daycare center should have requirements for the dogs who go there, including proof of vaccinations, a health evaluation, and a behavioral screening. Also ask about what they do when two dogs don't get along, whether they have had any dogs injured at their facility and if so, why, and what the schedule is for the dogs.

When you can, drop in occasionally during the day unannounced, just to see how it's going. You should feel good about the place and the people who run it. You don't want to leave your beloved Beagle with just anyone, and you definitely want to be sure he is safe and well cared-for. Some daycare facilities will also board your Beagle for longer periods if you need to travel and can't take your Beagle along with you.

Helpful Hints

Can you take your Beagle to the office? More and more people work in pet-friendly places that allow well-behaved dogs to hang out on the job with their people. If you have the option and your Beagle won't be a distraction to you or others, taking your Beagle to work with you is a great way to spend more time together. Your Beagle won't be lonely and bored during the day, and will learn even more about the wide world. A good training class can go a long way toward preparing your Beagle for appropriate behavior in the work-place, so make sure you sign up.

Traveling with a Beagle

Sooner or later, you're probably going to need to go on a trip, even if you'd rather stay home and dote on your Beagle puppy all day. Obviously, you can't always travel with a pet, but when you have the option, taking your Beagle along for the ride can be fun for everyone. Your Beagle will get to experience more of the world (more socialization), and you'll have your best buddy at your side.

Traveling with a Beagle requires preparation. You can't just throw him in your suitcase and hit the road. The selectively deaf, escape-artist Beagle requires some precautions, and traveling without preparation can make the trip unpleasant for everyone.

First, consider whether your Beagle can handle the trip.

- Has he been through obedience class? If not, he may not be well-behaved enough and could disturb you and others.
- Is he nervous about the car? Lots of short fun car rides with treat rewards can help get your Beagle used to the car, and it's a good idea to do this before you hit the road for a ten-hour day of driving.
- Is he healthy? Some dogs with health problems can't take the stress of travel, and it can worsen their condition. Get the thumbs-up from your veterinarian before hitting the road.
- Does he have the necessary vaccinations? If you plan to leave the country, be sure you know exactly what you need to do if you are bringing

your pet. He will need documentation of his health and vaccinations, and may need to endure a quarantine period.

- Can you drive, or do you have to fly? Beagle puppies are small enough to ride in the cabin of an airplane with you, but larger Beagles would probably have to travel by cargo. You will have to pay extra to fly with a dog, and every airline has individual rules that apply to pet travelers. Although some dogs travel by air with no problem, being treated as baggage can be pretty rough on more sensitive dogs, or those that aren't in perfect health. Even the most self-assured Beagle could come out of the cargo hold feeling shaken. In a few unfortunate cases, pets have perished in the cargo hold, or escaped from their crates. Consider the risks before making the decision.
- Do you have room for all the supplies you will need on the road like the crate, food and water, bowls, toys, and the leash?

Helpful Hints

These web sites will help you find pet-friendly lodging for your trip. Always call first to be sure the policy hasn't changed.

- Pets Welcome
  www.petswelcome.com
- Official Pet Hotels
  www.officialpethotels.com
- Dog Friendly
  www.dogfriendly.com
- Travel Pets
  www.travelpets.com

BE PREPARED! Beagles on the Go

When you do decide to travel with your Beagle, make certain you have all the supplies you will need on the road. Remember, Beagles cannot be trusted off-leash, and are good at escaping to follow a scent trail. At the very least, you will need to take the following supplies with you.

- Crate. Bring along your Beagle's regular crate, so he always has somewhere familiar to go, no matter where he is. Some types of crates are collapsible so they don't take up the whole trunk, which is really nice for frequent travelers.
- Collar with identification tags, which your Beagle should wear at all times.
- A sturdy leash.
- Dog seatbelt or crate that can be belted into the car.
- Enough of your dog's regular food to last the trip.
- A jug of the water your dog normally drinks. (As with people, dogs can get ill drinking water they aren't used to drinking.)
- A couple of your dog's favorite toys, including things to chew. Chewing is a great stress-reliever.
- Your dog's regular treats. Try not to vary what he eats and drinks too much during a trip, to minimize stress and stomach upset.
- Dog bed, if your dog sleeps in one separate from his crate.
- Medications your dog requires, including any pest control products he might need.
- Vaccination and other medical records from your veterinarian. If you are traveling by air or crossing a border, these will probably be required.
- Bags and scoop to pick up after your dog.

You should also make arrangements ahead of time. Not all hotels and motels accept dogs. Reserve in advance, inform them you will be bringing a dog, and be prepared to pay a deposit against any damage. Some hotels require a nonrefundable pet and/or cleaning fee.

Also call ahead to national parks, trails, beaches, and other travel destinations, to find out whether or not dogs are welcome. You don't want to drive your Beagle all the way across the country, only to find out you can't do anything you had planned on doing because you have a dog in tow. AAA publishes an annual book called *Traveling With Your Pet*, which lists thousands of pet-friendly, AAA-rated lodgings and campgrounds. Or check out the many web sites on-line that maintain lists of pet-friendly travel spots.

If you decide it just isn't possible or practical to take your Beagle with you, you will need to make arrangements for someone to take care of him. Some people have family or friends that willingly let their Beagles "sleep over" while they are gone, but those without that option will need to hire a professional who is trained for the job.

Pet Sitters

Pet sitting has become a booming industry. According to Pet Sitters International, it's among the fastest growing of home-based businesses. No matter where you live, chances are that at least one and probably several people near you work as full-time or part-time pet sitters.

Professionals are often veterinary technicians who are insured and bonded, but expect to pay. Pet-sitting visits can range from $10 to $20 or higher for a 30-minute visit, and cost much more for overnight stays. Yet, you are paying for quality. Professional pet sitters should be trained in animal first aid, should know how to administer medication, and should have knowledge of how to interact with animals and deal with any crisis that may occur. Pet sitters with fewer professional qualifications may cost less, and some responsible college students also pet sit. If you are comfortable and find someone who really bonds with your Beagle, a non-pro could turn out to be a great option. If you want to go with the professionals, look up "pet sitters" in your phone book or consult an online service such as Pet Sitters International (*www.petsit.com*) or the National Association of Professional Pet Sitters (*www.petsitters.org*). A good professional pet sitter is worth her weight in kibble.

Helpful Hints

Pet sitters do more than just watch your pets when you go on vacation. If you have to be at work all day, they can come to your house over the lunch hour to walk your Beagle, or just take him out in the yard and play with him. Since Beagles shouldn't stay confined in a crate for more than four hours, pet sitters are a great option for those who can't escape the office midday.

Boarding

The days of the Spartan boarding kennel are fading away, as these no-frills facilities are replaced with kinder, gentler, and plusher accommodations and more attention for dogs, including yards to romp in, agility equipment to navigate, and special services like grooming. Some of these facilities are also doggy daycare or dog spa facilities. Dogs may still sleep in kennels, but they can bring all the comforts of home. Many provide cushy dog beds and other luxuries, even televisions, grooming services, training sessions, and pet massage! Some have on-staff veterinarians, and staff should be trained in how to handle squabbles between dogs and other behavior problems.

If you think your friendly Beagle would enjoy hanging out with other dogs and running around a big yard while you are gone (and what

Beagle wouldn't?), look into this type of facility. Check out the place before leaving your Beagle there, though. If you don't like the looks of it or get a bad feeling, pass. If the place looks like dog heaven and the staff is well trained, then your Beagle may just get to take his own vacation.

To find a facility, look up "pet boarding" or "dog services" in your phone book, or ask your local veterinarian for recommendations.

Disaster Preparedness

When Hurricane Katrina struck New Orleans in 2005, hundreds of Beagles and Beagle mixes lost their homes, and Beagle rescue groups all over the country took in these lost Beagles, to help find them new homes. Most were never returned to their owners, and many were already strays in the city. You may not like to think about a natural disaster hitting your home and affecting your family, but it certainly could happen. Hurricanes may be risks primarily in coastal areas and earthquakes may generally affect only those areas near fault lines, but almost anywhere in the United States could be subject to the ravages of tornadoes, floods, fire, toxic waste spills, or terrorist acts. You know what they say: Better safe than sorry, and that applies not only to you and your family but to your Beagle. If you have the necessary supplies and know-how in case of evacuation, you can drastically minimize the chances that you and your Beagle will be separated during a disaster.

Every single pet in your home needs to have a carrier that it could live in temporarily, in case of evacuation. That means your Beagle's crate, so if you don't have one yet or don't want to use one at home, at least have one in case of emergencies. If your Beagle is used to the crate, it will be much more comforting during high-stress times when your Beagle must be inside it. Even if you don't crate-train or your Beagle doesn't sleep in a crate, it's a good idea to keep it somewhere in the house, with the door open, a blanket inside, and maybe a few treats, so it is at least familiar to your Beagle. He might not go inside very much, but at least he will know what it is. If you have other dogs, cats, small animals, or any other pet, they should each have a carrier, too, just in case. Keep them in the garage or storage area in the basement if you must, but have them somewhere easily accessible . . . just in case.

Other items to keep easily accessible, preferably in some kind of container that you can grab and go, include:

- Extra food and water bowls
- A stash of fresh food (switch it out regularly)
- Extra medication your Beagle needs (switch it out regularly so it doesn't expire)

- Bottled water
- Water purification tablets
- Sanitation bags
- A few toys
- Extra collar with ID tags
- Extra leash
- Extra brush, comb, nail clippers, and any other necessary grooming supplies
- Copy of your Beagle's vaccination and medical records
- Written information about your Beagle's regular feeding schedule, medication schedule, any medical problems, behavioral problems, and any other special needs your Beagle has, in case someone else has to take care of him
- A list and description of all the animals you have in your house, in case someone has to go back and find a missing pet
- A card with important contact information written on it, including the names, addresses, and phone numbers of your veterinarian, veterinary emergency clinic, boarding facility, hotel or motel outside of town, friends and family who can help
- Basic first aid: antibiotic ointment, steroid cream, bandages, gauze, adhesive tape, rubbing alcohol, styptic powder to stop bleeding, iodine, surgical scissors, and anything else your veterinarian recommends for your particular dog. Put all the first aid equipment in a plastic box or tub and label it.
- Rope
- Clean towel
- Blanket
- Flashlight
- Light stick

If you have all these supplies assembled and ready to go, someone else can grab them if you aren't able to get back home in an emergency. It's a very good idea to have a back-up plan, in case you can't get home during a disaster. Who can you designate to go to your house, get your Beagle (and any other pets), and grab your supplies? Arrange this ahead of time, and be someone else's back-up plan, too, in case they can't get home to their own pets. If you are separated, where will you meet? Tell your designated person where the carriers and disaster kit are located, so they can find everything quickly. If your animals tend to hide in a specific place when they are nervous, tell your designated person that information, too. Give them extra copies of your lists and information cards, just in case, and take extra copies of theirs. You also might want to swap extra house keys, so your Beagle doesn't end up locked inside your house.

I sincerely hope you will never need to use your disaster kit, but just in case, you will be ready, and your Beagle will have the best chance possible of staying healthy and not getting separated from—or eventually getting returned to—you.

Communicating with Your Beagle

Voice Beagles may not act like they are listening to you, but believe it or not, they are perfectly capable of perceiving the slightest change in your voice. Say "Do you want to go for a walk?" with enthusiasm, and that will mean something entirely different than saying those same words in a gloomy monotone voice. Modulation of your voice will let your Beagle know whether you are happy or displeased with his behavior. In fact, he can determine changes in voice better than *you* can because he has such a fine-tuned sense of hearing, so when you let your own problems sneak into your Beagle talk, your dog may mistake your sad or irritated feelings as a message that he is doing something wrong. In other words, when you speak to your Beagle, let your voice reflect the message you want him to get. As for shouting, don't bother. You don't need to be so obvious. A slightly annoyed or disapproving tone is all you need for your Beagle to get the message that he is not doing as he should. You can tell by your Beagle's "guilty" expression that he knows exactly what you are talking about. You can also tell, when your Beagle becomes enthusiastic and responsive, that he knows you are praising him. Of course, a treat helps to reinforce that message.

Hands Beagles may not see as well as you see, but they do detect movement and outlines pretty well, so hand signals can be a useful adjunct to vocal cues. Many Beagles learn cues, such as stay, dance, or roll over, solely by hand signals. You may not even need to use words, although using both reinforces the message. Some hand signals, such as the ones for "down," "stay," "over," and "come," are essential for competitive dog sports like obedience (granted, not the Beagle's forte). You can also use hand signals in your training at home, to send your Beagle to fetch something, find something, or go to his kennel. As with vocal cues, use treats to reinforce good behavior, so your Beagle will know exactly when he gets the right message and does the right thing.

Facial Expressions Oh, those sad Beagle eyes! That pleading expression! And that furrowed brow! Beagles can have pretty expressive faces, and sometimes you can tell what your Beagle is thinking by the position of his eyes and ears. Is he ready to play? (Ears forward, eyes smiling.) Hot on the trail? (Head down, brow furrowed.) Waiting intently for a piece of food to fall to the floor? (Head up, eyes wide open.) Worried? (Brow furrowed, head back.) Frightened? (Eyes wide, ears back.) While body postures and tail set are also indicative of a Beagle's mood, just looking into your Beagle's eyes can tell you quite a bit about his current state of mind.

Body Movement

Beagles offer major clues to their mood via their body language, so watch how your Beagle reacts physically to different situations, and you'll get better at reading him. For example, when a Beagle is happy, wants to play, or wants attention from you, he is likely to wiggle his whole body, wag his tail, or bow down to get you engaged. When he lowers his head and eyes, sinks down or lies down on the floor, or cowers, he is unhappy, upset, or afraid. When his hackles rise, he is on full alert and senses dangers or intrusion. A stiff body, growling, and snarling translate to fighting mode, which is rare for a Beagle but can happen if he feels he or his family are threatened. When he rolls over and bares his belly, he is being trusting or submissive.

Scents

Now we're talking a language your Beagle *really* understands: the language of smell. Dogs can all detect scent better than humans, but Beagles are better at scent detection than many other dog breeds. They can follow a scent trail for miles, so they can certainly find hidden treats, not to mention that crumb in the bottom of the kitchen trash can or that last crust of sandwich on the plate you left on the counter (and don't think he can't get up there). Scent means more to dogs than it does to humans. To the extent that we can see, they can smell, and Beagles "see" the world through their noses in a very real way. To your Beagle, you are a particular scent, even more than you are a particular shape, and that scent means home, security, and affection. Remember, also, that food is foremost on a Beagle's mind and he can find it anywhere, so watch where you leave things and keep your Beagle protected from things he might smell but should never eat, such as spoiled food or antifreeze.

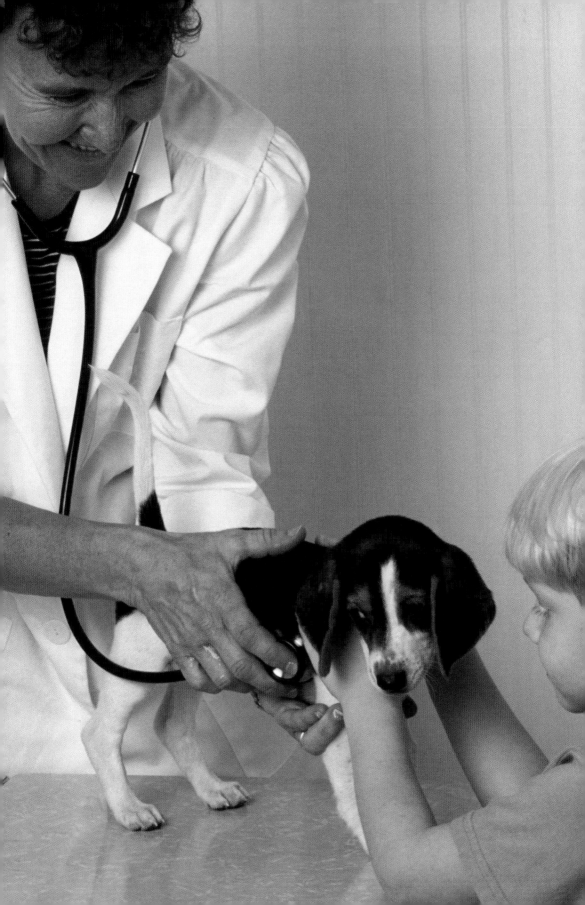

Chapter Six

Health and Nutrition

From his very first puppy check-up to his very last senior check-up, your Beagle depends on you to make sure he gets good health care. He also depends on you for good meals—and the more the better, as far as he's concerned. You can go to just any veterinarian and buy just any bag of dog food, but wouldn't you rather make the best choices for your Beagle?

The bottom line, when it comes to keeping pets healthy, is to make sure they lead a healthy life. Beagles need high-quality food, daily vigorous exercise, and regular grooming. They also need socialization, training, and lots of interaction with friendly humans. They need a fenced yard and a sturdy leash, to keep them out of harm's way, and they need regular veterinary care, including vaccinations, to head off health problems in the future and to quickly resolve any that might arise.

Beagles also need to be Beagles. Respect the hound! Beagles need to exercise their scenting ability, stretch their legs, and exert themselves. They need to have physical and mental challenges, the opportunity to think independently, and the chance to explore the world safely, with you on the other end of the leash.

Practice these basic principles, and you should have a healthy, happy Beagle.

However, it helps to know a little more, such as how to find a good veterinarian, what health issues sometimes plague Beagles, and how to choose a good food for your hungry dog. Let's start with your number-one ally when it comes to keeping your Beagle healthy: Your veterinarian.

Finding the Right Veterinarian

If you have other pets, you probably already have a veterinarian, but if this is your first dog, or if you haven't had a pet in a long time, you may need to find one. Most towns and cities have many veterinarians to choose from, so while you can certainly visit the vet closest to where you live, you might benefit from shopping around.

Get recommendations from friends, especially those with Beagles, or ask your local breeder for a recommendation. When you take your Beagle puppy in for his very first check-up, you'll also have a chance to check out the veterinarian. If you aren't comfortable with her style, feel rushed, or don't think she relates very well to your dog, you can certainly switch veterinarians. Call some other places and try them out. You shouldn't settle for anything less than the best veterinarian for your Beagle, and sometimes it's worthwhile to drive a little farther for one you and your Beagle really like.

The First Check-up

When you first take your Beagle to the veterinarian, she will typically give your Beagle a physical exam, feeling all over to make sure everything is in the right place. Does your Beagle look healthy and normal? She'll let you know. She will also weigh your Beagle and record his weight, to make sure he is growing properly.

If the breeder hasn't already done it, the veterinarian will also give your Beagle his first or second set of vaccinations. Every veterinarian has a vaccination schedule they recommend, and they aren't exactly the same. Ask your veterinarian how often she recommends vaccinating your puppy. Some people believe in vaccinating less often, especially after the first year. If you are worried about excessive vaccinations, talk to your veterinarian about the benefits versus the risks. She is almost certainly aware of the issue, and can tell you about your options and which vaccinations are required by law (rabies, for example).

Breed Truths

Because of their manageable size and laid-back temperaments, Beagles are the breed of dog used most widely in laboratory testing. While this is certainly unfortunate for Beagles and upsetting to many people who live with companion animals, the positive side is that Beagles have been so thoroughly studied that we know more about Beagle health than the health of just about any other breed. While some vets don't have much experience with rarer breeds, most know a lot about Beagles, and the scientific literature is full of plenty of accessible information about them.

Also ask which vaccinations are particularly necessary in your area. Most veterinarians give standard core vaccines for diseases like parvovirus and distemper. Some others will also recommend vaccinations for parainfluenza, bordetella, Lyme disease, and leptospirosis, if those diseases are a problem in your area. The rabies virus is typically administered at 4 to 6 months of age.

The veterinarian will probably give your puppy a deworming treatment, which is standard for new puppies. She will probably also give your Beagle a heartworm test and a supply of heartworm medication. Almost any Beagle that spends time outside should be on regular preventive heartworm medication to prevent potentially fatal heartworms that can be transmitted through mosquito bites. This is also a good time to talk to your veterinarian about flea and tick control. If you live in a flea-prone or tick-prone area, you may want to start

BE PREPARED! Vaccination Schedules

Every veterinarian has a vaccination schedule she typically recommends. It will probably look something like this:

- Core vaccine at 6–8 weeks: Parvovirus, distemper, adenovirus, and possibly parainfluenza and bordetella.
- Second core vaccine at 10–12 weeks: The veterinarian may also add leptospirosis or Lyme disease vaccines if these diseases are common in your area.
- Third core vaccine at 14–16 weeks.
- Rabies vaccine at 16–24 weeks.
- Annual core vaccine booster at 1 year.
- Core vaccine boosters every 1 to 3 years after the first year, or as recommended by your veterinarian.

your Beagle on a preventive product right away. Your veterinarian can recommend and provide you with a good one.

The first veterinarian visit also gives her a chance to meet your new Beagle and make notes about him, so that if anything changes in the future, she'll have something for comparison.

Beagle Health Issues

Beagles are generally healthy, sound dogs that rarely get sick. However, every purebred dog has certain conditions it can be prone to developing, and the Beagle is no exception.

Common Conditions

Although any dog can develop any disease, the following conditions are slightly more common in Beagles than in some other breeds. (These conditions are listed alphabetically, not in order of how common or severe they are.)

Demodetic Mange This nasty skin condition is caused by a mite that burrows under the skin. It can result in bacterial infections of the skin and significant hair loss. Symptoms include crusty, scaly skin; intense itching; skin irritation and swelling; and skin darkening. A veterinarian can treat mange to kill the mites. Related skin infections may also need antibiotics.

Dwarfism and Other Skeletal Disorders A well-built Beagle is shorter than a Foxhound, but shouldn't be a dwarfed dog. However, sometimes, Beagle puppies are born with skeletal abnormalities that can result in a wide range of strangely shaped Beagles. Some look completely normal except for super-short legs, like a Dachshund. Some have very short tails. Other skeletal abnormalities include extremely small Beagles that don't develop normally, or Beagles with cleft lips or palates, slanted eyes, or crooked front legs and backs. Some of these dogs will have serious health problems because of their skeletal disorders, while others end up perfectly healthy, if a bit unusual in appearance.

Epilepsy Epilepsy is a seizure disorder, and can be mild or severe. Nobody knows for sure what causes epilepsy, but there is probably a genetic component in Beagles, especially in those that develop epilepsy during the first year. Symptoms of a seizure include stiffened muscles, falling over, jerking motions, loss of bladder or bowel control, and involuntary noises. Most seizures last less than 2 minutes, and seizures sometimes occur in clusters. If you think your Beagle has had a seizure, call your veterinarian. Epilepsy can usually be managed fairly well with one or more medications, although sometimes it takes awhile to find out which medications work best on individual animals.

Eye Diseases and Disorders Many Beagles are prone to eye problems, and one of the most common is progressive retinal atrophy (PRA). This eye defect eventually results in blindness, so breeders are very careful not to breed dogs with this condition, and responsible breeders always test the parents of any litter to be sure they don't have this problem. However, every now and then, a Beagle will develop it, and if you get your Beagle from somewhere that doesn't test for PRA, your dog's risk of developing the disease will be higher.

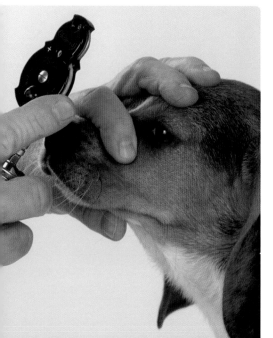

Other eye problems Beagles sometimes experience include abnormal location of eyelashes, which causes irritation to the eye; glaucoma, which is increased eyeball pressure resulting in pain and blindness if untreated with medication (even with medication, dogs with glaucoma often go blind); tear duct problems resulting in excessive tearing or dry eyes; and cherry eye, a condition in which an eye gland swells and protrudes from the eye. Cherry eye looks very disturbing but a veterinarian can easily fix the problem.

Hip Dysplasia Beagles don't develop hip dysplasia at the rate some larger breeds do, but some do suffer from this abnormal hip socket development that can cause rear-leg lameness and arthritis pain later in life.

Some cases are mild enough that they don't need any treatment. For others, your vet may recommend pain medication or even hip replacement surgery.

Hypothyroidism This autoimmune condition, in which the body attacks its own thyroid gland, can result in skin problems, hair loss, and excessive weight gain. Other symptoms sometimes include food allergies, ear infections, and dry eye syndrome. Your veterinarian can treat this condition with medication.

Intervertebral Disk Disease (IVDD or IDD) This condition results in spinal disk rupture, which can cause severe pain and, if untreated, rear-end paralysis. While it is more common in longer-backed dogs (Dachshunds are especially prone), Beagles can sometimes develop it. Signs of a disc rupture include sudden refusal or apparent inability to run, walk, or climb stairs, or a loud yelp of pain after jumping off furniture or when you touch the dog. Surgery within one or two days of a disc rupture can often restore function. Milder cases may require extended periods of inactivity, during which your Beagle must be confined to a crate for several weeks (except for bathroom breaks), so the spine can heal without further injury. Even with treatment, some dogs become permanently paralyzed. In the past, vets often recommended euthanizing paralyzed dogs but today, many people live happily with their paraplegic pets, who get around nicely with little carts to support their rear ends.

Patellar Luxation Luxating patellas are kneecaps that slip out of place because of a faulty joint or an injury. Suspect this condition if your Beagle suddenly stops using one leg and hops along with the leg lifted up in the air. This disorder is more common in toy breeds, but Beagles can sometimes develop it. Many can live with it. Severe cases can be corrected with a simple surgery.

If you suspect your Beagle may be suffering from these or any other health problems, never hesitate to give your veterinarian a call. It's always better to check out a potential problem than to ignore it until it is too late.

Helpful Hints

For more information on living with a pet that has IVDD, see Dodgers List: *www.dodgerslist.com*. This site offers information and support for people with dogs with spinal disc ruptures, as well as support for people living and caring for paralyzed dogs. While many Dachshund owners frequent the site, other breeds are also represented, including Beagles.

Holistic/Complementary Care for Beagles

A decade ago, few people knew anything about holistic health care, let alone practiced it. Today, however, as people become increasingly concerned about their own health, rising medical costs, and the effects of drugs and chemicals on the human body, they are turning to more natural or nontraditional health care, from herbal medicine and homeopathy to chiropractic care and acupuncture. And, as often happens when humans get interested in something for themselves, they then turn to the same things for their pets. If glucosamine can make your achy joints feel better, can it do the same thing for your Beagle? If a massage makes you feel better, wouldn't your arthritic Beagle enjoy one, too?

More doctors and veterinarians are training in holistic healing techniques, and even conventional doctors and veterinarians are beginning to recommend certain nontraditional approaches to healing, as those approaches are increasingly supported by sound research. For instance, studies show that the supplement glucosamine really does help some people and pets with pain and stiffness from arthritis.

Should you consider holistic or complementary care for your Beagle? Maybe, but the best method is probably to investigate alternative health care with the guidance of your regular veterinarian. Many veterinarians today are happy to work with holistic practitioners, providing pets with the best of both worlds.

What Is Holistic/Complementary Health Care?

Holistic comes from the word "whole," and it is an approach to health that looks at the whole person or animal, rather than an isolated disease or symptom. For example, if your Beagle has itchy skin, a holistic veterinarian will look at the skin, but not just the skin. He might ask what your Beagle is eating, how much he is sleeping, how he is acting, how *you* are acting. Have you changed his diet? Is he getting exercise, and enough attention? Have

CAUTION

The terms "holistic" and "natural" are hot in the pet product market these days, and an increasing concern about the environment has fueled the natural health trend, so that pet products are now sporting buzzwords like *natural*, *organic*, *eco-friendly*, and *green*. Manufacturers know that these words appeal to many people, but because these terms aren't always regulated, some less reputable manufacturers use them indiscriminately. It's important to know what you are buying. Just because a product is natural or eco-friendly doesn't necessarily mean it is safer or better for your pet, and just because a product says it is something doesn't mean it really is. Research products before you buy, talk to knowledgeable pet store owners about the products they choose to stock, even call up the companies with your questions. Knowledge is power and a skeptical consumer is a safer and wiser one.

you started cleaning your carpets with a new chemical, or washed his bedding with a new detergent? Is there a new stressor in the home, such as a move or a new pet?

In other words, every aspect of your Beagle's life, from a holistic point of view, can impact every other aspect. Disease isn't isolated. It is the result of an imbalance within the entire system, so to correct the disease, the holistic healer tries to balance the system. Once balanced, the body will fix its own problems.

Complementary health care utilizes the best of both worlds. Conventional veterinary care is important for emergency situations (like a broken bone) and acute conditions (like a spinal disc rupture or a serious bacterial infection).

Holistic approaches work best for chronic conditions, from allergies and arthritis to obesity. Holistic approaches tend to avoid pharmaceuticals, in favor of slower-acting but safer and more natural remedies such as herbs, as well as adjustments to the Beagle's diet, exercise, and schedule.

To help jump-start your research into the many kinds of holistic therapies, here is a brief description of some of the more common holistic/complementary approaches being applied to pets.

CAUTION

Because "holistic" is trendy right now but not a legally defined term, anyone can use it to describe anything they are doing. Be as choosy about your holistic health practitioner as you would be about your regular veterinarian. Any holistic health practitioner should have extensive training, be reputable in the field, and should be able to provide you with references.

Nutritional Therapy

When thousands of pets were poisoned by tainted pet food in 2007, the average consumer suddenly became more aware of what might be in a bag of pet food. However, that wasn't the beginning of nutritional therapy. Long before the tragic pet food scandal, holistically oriented veterinarians and even pet food manufacturers advised improving a pet's diet to improve a pet's health. Cheap dog food contains a lot of artificial ingredients and fillers—the equivalent of a diet of cheap fast food for humans. Some dogs get by okay on these foods, but others develop many food-related health problems, from skin allergies to gastrointestinal problems to (some say) cancer.

Many holistic health practitioners say that the first thing any pet owner should do to improve a pet's health is to feed a better diet. Whether that includes dog food made of high quality natural ingredients, a home-cooked diet, or even a carefully formulated diet of raw food, the gist behind nutritional therapy is that we all really are what we eat. Most holistic veterinarians agree that a pet's diet is extremely important for overall health. For more on what to feed your Beagle, see the section on pet food at the end of this chapter.

Supplements

Conventional wisdom says that a high-quality dog food is all the nutrition your dog needs, but that wisdom is giving way to the notion that individually tweaking an animal's system with the right remedies might maximize health. The main kinds of supplements available for animals today include:

Dietary Supplements/Nutraceuticals These supplements could fill in nutritional gaps your dog's food misses. Some include live enzymes and probiotics your pet would get if he ate raw food in the wild, to make up for what processed kibble lacks. Some include ingredients like glucosamine, for stronger and more flexible joints, or essential fatty acids, for healthier skin and coat. Your holistic veterinarian can recommend appropriate supplements for your Beagle's individual needs. Some knowledgeable retail pet store owners specializing in holistic products may also be able to make recommendations for you. To find companies that are members of the National Animal Supplement Council—an organization that requires members to follow high standards of quality in manufacturing and advertising their products—visit the National Animal Supplement Council web site at *http://nasc.cc*.

Herbal Supplements and Chinese Herbs Usually gentler and slower-acting than chemical pharmaceuticals, herbal remedies may help resolve many medical problems in pets, and/or support healthy functioning of organ systems. These may come in pills, powders, or liquid, and may be made of individual herbs (like valerian or chamomile, for calming) or combinations of herbs (such as ginger, mint, and fennel, for upset stomachs). A qualified herbalist or holistic veterinarian can advise you about what herbs would be appropriate for your Beagle. For more information about herbal remedies, I like the book *All You Ever Wanted to Know About Herbs for Pets*, by Mary L. Wulff-Tilford and Gregory L. Tilford.

Homeopathic Remedies Homeopathy is a method for balancing the body's health through the concept of "like cures like." Substances known to cause symptoms in large doses are drastically diluted into harmless remedies that spark a healing reaction with a body experiencing those same symptoms. While homeopathy sounds counter-intuitive, plenty of people believe it works, and have the stories to back up their claims.

Flower Essences Flower essences are waters that have been infused with the essences of different flowers. They are for healing on an energetic rather than physical level, and many people swear they help balance emotionally distraught or stressed-out pets. Rescue Remedy is one of the most popular flower essences for stress reduction. You can give it to your anxious Beagle during a thunderstorm, and even take it yourself.

Pet Physical Therapies

Holistic veterinarians and other health practitioners are using many of the same physical therapies on pets that humans have been using for years. These therapies manipulate the physical body or the energetic body to balance the system, so the body can heal itself.

Acupuncture Used to treat everything from joint pain to kidney failure, acupuncture has many fans. People say it decreases pain and other uncomfortable symptoms in pets, even though western researchers don't really know why it works. This ancient practice involves inserting ultra-thin needles into certain parts of the body. Surprisingly, most pets don't seem to mind.

Chiropractic Care Many people swear by their chiropractor, and an increasing number also claim great benefits for their pets after visiting a veterinary chiropractor, who manipulates the body to re-align it for better health and healing.

Pet Massage Many pets truly enjoy a good massage, and you can give your Beagle a massage at home. However, if your Beagle has an orthopedic problem, regular massages by a professional pet massage therapist, using any of several massage and bodywork methods (including energy work like Reiki that manipulates a pet's energy field rather than physical body), might reduce pain and increase mobility. Some animal massage therapists also do chiropractic adjustments and/or energy healing. Be sure the therapist you choose is well trained.

Beagle Nutrition

Enough about the veterinarian, your Beagle might be thinking. When is it time to *eat?* Food is a serious priority for Beagles, and choosing the right food is an important priority for the person feeding the Beagle.

Your breeder probably sent you home with a little bit of the food she was feeding your Beagle, and you may want to stick with this food. If you can't find the right food or you want to upgrade, you have a lot of options. How do you know which one is right for your Beagle? Forget the pretty package and the expensive marketing. You need to know what's really in that food, to be sure you make the right choice.

Kibble, Canned, or Homemade?

Commercial pet food comes in two types: kibble (dry) or canned (wet). Each has its pros and cons. Kibble is less expensive, stays fresher longer, and may provide some tooth-cleaning benefits. Canned tastes better to some dogs, and looks more like real food to people. A little bit of canned food mixed with kibble can make kibble more appealing, but canned food is a lot more expensive and you have to keep opened cans in the refrigerator so the food doesn't spoil.

Some breeds are pretty picky, and need canned food to jazz up their kibble, or they won't be interested. Beagles aren't one of those breeds. While individual Beagles may occasionally have a more discerning palate, most of them will eat anything and everything you put in front of them. In other words, your Beagle's choosiness probably won't factor into the decision, so it's really up to you. A more important consideration is the quality of the food you choose, whether it is wet or dry.

What about home-prepared diets? Some people argue that commercial pet food is too processed and dogs should eat a home-cooked or even a raw diet. Others don't trust commercial pet food to be safe, and feel more comfortable feeding their pets the food they eat. Some vets agree, and some don't.

Commercial pet food is carefully formulated to be nutritionally complete, and many dogs fed a homemade diet lack important nutrients. It is, however, highly processed. Home-prepared raw diets could be hazardous because of bacterial contamination in raw meat, which can affect your dog as well as you (the preparer) and children in the house, who might touch the food. Raw diets that include raw bones could also be hazardous—many dogs have fractured teeth while chewing bones.

However, many dogs thrive on a home-cooked or raw diet, and some dogs with serious health problems have enjoyed greatly increased health and the complete resolution of symptoms such as skin problems after switching to a raw diet. Whether or not you are willing to do the work to research how to feed these kinds of diets to your dog, and take the time to make the food yourself, is up to you. Consider the options, but proceed with caution.

Helpful Hints

A steadily increasing number of pet food companies are now manufacturing raw-food diets for pets. If you like the idea of a raw diet but just don't have the time or energy to do it yourself, these products can be a great alternative.

Assessing Pet Food Quality

A high-quality pet food is important for your Beagle's health. Many dogs on cheap food develop itchy skin, excessive shedding, loose stools, and other unpleasant problems. Dogs on a high-quality food tend to have smaller, firmer stools and softer, shinier coats. Plus, cheap food isn't really a bargain. It contains so many fillers that you need to feed a lot more food each day. Premium food is the real bargain.

But once you get up into the premium category (the more expensive foods), how do you know which one to pick? Most premium foods are adequate to keep a Beagle healthy, but they also vary quite a bit. You can choose one that your veterinarian recommends. Or, get really choosy and consider a few additional things:

- **Taste:** If your dog doesn't like it and won't eat it, it doesn't matter how good a food it is. (Although, as I already mentioned, most Beagles will eat anything.)
- **Nutritional content:** Is the food formulated for your dog? All foods

FYI: Animal By-products

Animal by-products are non-muscle-meat parts of the animal used in pet food. These could include clean animal heads, feet, organs, blood, intestines, and fat. Logic suggests that by-products are natural food for dogs, since in the wild, a dog would probably eat most of an animal. However, many people avoid by-products in pet foods because foods are not required to tell you exactly what parts of the animals are included. Lately, there has been a trend in food and treats to leave out by-products. If you don't like the idea of by-products in your Beagle's food (and if you don't, you aren't alone), look for foods and treats with the "no by-products" claim on the front and read the ingredients label on the back to be sure the product is by-product free.

designed to be complete diets for dogs should state that feeding tests prove that the food meets the Association of Animal Feed Control Officials (AAFCO) standards for adult dogs or for puppies, depending on the formula you choose. They must meet minimum standards for protein, fat, fiber, and moisture, and contain all the necessary nutrients to keep dogs healthy. In addition, some foods are formulated specifically for seniors, overweight dogs, or canine athletes.

CAUTION

If a dog food is soft and chewy, you can bet it contains a lot of artificial ingredients, including sweetener, to make it that way. These semi-soft foods are junk food for dogs and best avoided. Canned food should be soft and kibble should be crunchy.

- **Ingredients:** Look at the ingredients label. High-quality pet foods are made mostly of high-quality protein sources like fresh meat. Foods that are primarily made of grains like corn and wheat are not as high in quality because dogs can't digest the proteins from grains as efficiently as they digest the protein from meat. Foods that also contain fruits, vegetables, fish oils, and other ingredients you recognize also may be higher in quality. Look carefully at the words you don't recognize, however. They may be artificial ingredients, or they may be the long names for added vitamins and minerals. More dog foods today are improving their ingredients lists by clearly defining what is in the food.
- **Organic or natural?:** Natural foods can't be made with artificial preservatives. Foods labeled as organic must contain 95 percent certified organic ingredients, and foods that say they are "made with organic ingredients" must contain at least 70 percent organic ingredients. Some companies try to get around these rules or use the words illegally

because pet food label claims aren't always enforced strictly. Plus, research hasn't proven that organic foods are any more nutritious than those that are conventionally grown. Whether or not you believe organic ingredients make a difference to your pet's (or the earth's) health, foods made with natural and especially organic ingredients tend to contain higher-quality ingredients. They also cost more, but for many people, the improved quality and absence of possibly health-altering chemical ingredients is worth the extra cost. Your call.

- **Bells and whistles:** Many foods promote the addition of "special" ingredients such as glucosamine for joint health or probiotics for better digestion. Supplements are better sources for these ingredients because you can be sure your dog actually gets enough of them to do some good. A miniscule dose of glucosamine or probiotics probably won't make any difference to your Beagle, but you may pay for it with a higher price tag. Then again, if you find a really good food that happens to contain glucosamine or probiotics or other supplemental ingredients, there's no reason to put it back on the shelf.

Monitoring Your Beagle's Weight

The most common chronic health problem in pets is obesity, and Beagles are one of the breeds most prone to packing on the pounds. While, weight gain may be a result of a medical problem like hypothyroidism, it's more likely that your Beagle is overweight because he is getting too much food and too little exercise.

Your Beagle isn't going to push away the food bowl with a "No thanks, I'm trying to cut down." It's up to you to make sure your Beagle stays at a healthy weight.

If you have a growing puppy, feed him a good high-quality puppy food, but don't feed him too much. The pet food bag will guide you in the amount you should feed your puppy according to age and size, but those amounts are often too high. Start your puppy on the low-end of the range suggested, and that should probably be plenty. Your veterinarian can help you monitor your puppy's weight to be sure he is growing properly.

If you have an adult Beagle, take a good hard look at him from the side and from above. Does he have a nice tuck-up in the stomach area and does his waist curve in slightly from his ribs? Can you feel, but not see, his ribs when you

run your hands along his sides? If so, he's probably just fine. If he looks like a sausage, his belly hangs, and you can't feel any sign of a rib cage, he's probably overweight.

Your veterinarian can help you determine whether your Beagle has a weight problem, and can help you deal with how to handle that problem, but the easiest thing to do is to prevent obesity in the first place. Throughout your Beagle's life, err on the side of slightly smaller portions than the pet food bag recommends, supplement with healthy, low-calorie treats. Better yet, use pieces of your Beagle's regular kibble for training. Walk your Beagle every day, add a vigorous play session, and you'll keep him slim. Excess weight can contribute to or worsen many health problems as your Beagle ages, so please try to avoid this common Beagle pitfall. If you keep your Beagle at a healthy weight, he'll enjoy better health and mobility throughout his life.

Helpful Hints

Meal time may be over, but isn't it about time for a snack? Beagles love treats, and they make excellent training tools for the food-motivated Beagle. However, lots of treats contain junky ingredients. You feed your Beagle a high-quality food, why feed him junk-food treats? Instead, choose natural treats without added artificial ingredients, sweeteners, fillers, and by-products.

Chapter Seven

Training and Activities

As you and your Beagle settle into your routine and get to know each other, you may realize he needs more than a walk around the block and some dedicated television time. Remember, Beagles are born to run through the woods following a scent trail for hours at a time. Do you think your Beagle really wants to just sit there, slowly morphing into an overweight couch potato with painful joints and a laboring heart?

You already know your Beagle needs socialization and training, so what are you waiting for? There are great opportunities for Beagles to get physically and mentally active out there in the world. This chapter will help you find them.

Basic Training

Some say that hounds are nearly impossible to obedience-train and it's true that in the upper echelons of competitive obedience, you won't see many Beagles. (Okay, you probably won't see any.) You're more likely to see long lists of sporting breeds such as Golden and Labrador Retrievers, and herding breeds such as Border Collies and Shetland Sheepdogs, as well as the occasional precocious Poodle. That's because these breeds have been shaped over centuries to pay very close attention to everything their humans say, and respond accordingly.

Beagles? Not so much. Beagles are more independent thinkers. They might add your opinion into the mix, but they make their decisions based on what they smell and perceive about the situation. You say "sit?" What's in it for them? You say "stop barking!" If your Beagle could chuckle, he probably would, as if to say, "Yeah, that's a good one."

While hounds can be more challenging to train than some other breeds, many trainers point out that Beagles aren't actually difficult to obedience-train at all; you just need to use the right methods. Beagles love to do things, try new things, even practice old tricks if doing them correctly means getting a reward. That's why positive reinforcement is so important for training Beagles. Would you work if you didn't get a paycheck? Your Beagle wants a paycheck, too. Fortunately, paying a Beagle is as simple as tossing a treat and offering an appreciative pat on the rump or "Good dog!"

Any healthy, well-bred, well-socialized Beagle should be smart and motivated enough to learn all the basic obedience commands he needs to know to get along in life. Your Beagle should be able to sit, stay, lie down, come, get it, leave it, and walk nicely on a leash. Once you've both mastered these basics, you can get competitive with the sports in which Beagles are born and bred to excel. There is something amazing and inspiring about watching Beagles in the field, following their natural instincts as they track a scent trail, and there are plenty of ways to give your Beagle that chance.

Teaching Your Beagle the House Rules

Your Beagle won't be a good housemate if he constantly begs at the table, pulls on the leash, chews up your slippers, and jumps all over anybody who comes to visit. Beagles need to learn basic commands, such as

Helpful Hints

Caught in the Act!

One of the best ways to teach a Beagle to do something is to wait until he does it on his own, then praise him and mark the behavior with a word. You can push your Beagle into a *sit* all day long, but if you say "Sit" when he sits on his own, you will make a much bigger and longer-lasting impression. The independent Beagle will think it was all *his* idea, that wonderful thing he did that you praise him so lavishly for doing. You can teach your Beagle a lot of tricks this way. When he barks, say "Speak." When he stops barking, say "Shh." When he lies down, say "Down." When he jumps up, say "Jump." Catching your Beagle in the act of randomly doing things you want him to know how to do, then praising the heck out of him for being such an "obedient" dog, is much more effective than futilely saying a word like "Shh!" when your Beagle is doing something completely different, like barking. This training method is fun and works fast, but also requires that you watch your Beagle and use the cues as often as possible. If you only say "Sit" 10 percent of the time that he sits, he won't get the lesson as quickly.

sit, walk, leave it, down, and *come.* When you take your Beagle to puppy class, the instructor will probably introduce some of these commands, and give you some easy steps for teaching them to your Beagle, but don't wait for class to begin. Teach your Beagle the basics at home and practice two or three times a day for short periods. Young puppies can only concentrate for about five minutes, but as your Beagle gets older and more mature, he'll enjoy training for 15 minutes, 30 minutes, or even longer, provided you give him some interesting things to do.

Always keep a collar and leash on your Beagle during training, so he knows he's wearing his "uniform" and that means it's time to listen (and get

FYI: Clicker Training

Many dog trainers use clicker training, a highly effective, but sometimes misunderstood, method that originated with marine mammal trainers and is now applied to training situations for many different kinds of animals, from dogs and cats to rabbits and rats. The concept is simple and involves the use of a clicker—a small handheld device that makes a clicking sound at the press of a button.

To begin, every time the trainer gives the animal a treat or reward, she clicks the clicker. The animal quickly learns to associate the sound of the click with a reward. Then, during training sessions, every time the animal does something correctly, the trainer can precisely mark the correct behavior with a click. The treat comes after, but the clicker assures that the animal understands exactly which behavior is being rewarded. Clicker training works great for teaching pets basic behaviors, and for advanced training, it can result in very precise learning. It takes some practice to get the hang of it, however. If you are interested in clicker training your Beagle, look for a clicker training class in your area.

rewarded). Never practice for too long in one session; your Beagle will get bored and training won't be productive. If you start to get frustrated, give yourself a break and resume practice later. Training should always be fun for both you and your Beagle puppy. If it stays fun, you'll be surprised how quickly your Beagle will get on board with the whole training concept.

The *Down* Command

1. Begin by putting your Beagle puppy in front of you and showing him a treat.
2. Hold the treat in front of his nose, then slowly move it in a diagonal line towards the floor, away from the puppy. If he follows it by crouching or lying down, say "Down" and give him the treat and praise.
3. If he follows the treat but doesn't lie down, take the treat back to where you began. Do not give it to him until he does the right thing. This time, move the treat slowly away from him again as you very gently help guide him into a down position with your other hand, saying "Down."
4. When he is lying down, even if you have to hold him with your hand, give him the treat and praise him lavishly. Practice three or four times in a row, several times every day, until he understands what the word means and starts lying down on his own.

The *Come* Command

1. This cue is easy because puppies love to come to their people, especially people with treats. However, because Beagles are easily distracted, it pays off to practice this at least a few times every day. Begin by walking about four feet away from your Beagle puppy, treat in hand.
2. Crouch down, call your Beagle's name, and say, "Come!" If he isn't doing something more interesting, he will probably come to you right away. Give him the treat and praise him. If he doesn't come, keep coaxing him, or show him the treat, or try again later.
3. Do this often throughout the day, so he never knows when you might say "Come," and what wonderful prize might be waiting when he does.
4. You can involve the whole family in this game by putting the puppy in the middle of a circle of people, each with a treat. Take turns calling the puppy to "Come." If he comes to someone who didn't call, don't reward him. When he comes to the person who said "Come," give him the treat and praise.

The *Leave It* Command

1. The *leave it* command is useful when your Beagle has hold of something he isn't supposed to have, such as a shoe, a child's toy, or the remote control. Beagles don't like to give up what they have, unless they can trade it for something better, and that's the key to this cue. Begin by finding three different things your Beagle likes, each better than the other, such as a ball, a better toy, and a treat. Always save the food treat as the last item.

2. Give your Beagle the first toy and get him to take it in his mouth. If your puppy won't put the toy in his mouth, look for something else, or wait until he spontaneously picks up a toy with his mouth, and use that opportunity.

3. Show him the better toy as you say "Leave it," and take the first toy out of his mouth. Replace it with the second toy. Praise him.

4. Show him the treat as you say "Leave it" and take the second toy out of his mouth. Give him the treat. Praise him. Practice often with different items and he'll quickly learn that "Leave it" means "give it up and you'll get something better."

Basic Obedience Class

Once your Beagle graduates from puppy class, it's time to move on to a basic obedience class. Obedience class does more than teach your Beagle some basic commands. It also teaches *you* how to better communicate with your Beagle. Think of your obedience instructor as a translator helping you and your Beagle communicate in a language you both understand. She can help you figure out why you can't get your Beagle to lie down or walk on a leash, give you new helpful strategies, even help you tackle behavior problems your Beagle might be having. You can read every Beagle book ever published and still be stymied about how to handle a particular problem until an obedience instructor watches you and your Beagle in action. A good trainer can pinpoint what you and your Beagle might be doing wrong, in a way no book ever could.

But not all obedience instructors are great ones, or great with Beagles, so the first step is to find a class that is right for you and your hound. Your options will vary depending on where you live, but if you have the luxury of being choosy, talk to several instructors before signing up.

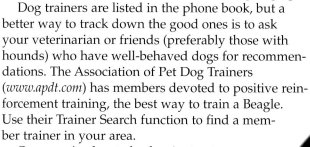

Dog trainers are listed in the phone book, but a better way to track down the good ones is to ask your veterinarian or friends (preferably those with hounds) who have well-behaved dogs for recommendations. The Association of Pet Dog Trainers (*www.apdt.com*) has members devoted to positive reinforcement training, the best way to train a Beagle. Use their Trainer Search function to find a member trainer in your area.

Once you've located a few instructors, make calls and see if you can observe a class, or just ask about the training methods and schedule. Some obedience instructors specialize in certain kinds of dogs, or certain kinds of situations. Look for teachers who offer basic obedience for pet owners using

BE PREPARED! Choosing an Obedience Instructor

Before you choose an obedience instructor, ask questions to be sure the methods used in class will be appropriate for you and your Beagle.

- Do you offer a basic obedience class for pet owners? What do you cover?
- Have you had a lot of hounds in your class? Do you have experience with Beagles?
- What is your training philosophy? Do you focus on positive reinforcement?
- Do you use choke collars?
- Do you encourage the use of food treats?
- Do you offer advanced classes that would be appropriate for Beagles, such as agility or tracking?

positive reinforcement methods including food treats, rather than punitive methods such as choke chains.

When you begin your classes, don't let that weekly session be the only time you and your Beagle work on the things you learn. Would you pay college tuition and never do your homework? Then why go to obedience class but never practice? Short daily practice sessions will make the most of your obedience class time. Be sure to ask your instructor about any problems you encounter at home so you don't inadvertently teach your Beagle the wrong behavior.

After you and your Beagle graduate from basic obedience, you can go on to other activities, such as earning a Canine Good Citizen certificate, or competing in agility, rally, tracking, hunt tests, or field trials.

Training Tests

You know your Beagle is a good citizen. Now, prove it to the world. Your Beagle can earn an American Kennel Club Canine Good Citizen (CGC) certificate by passing a 10-step test to show he has good manners and knows how to behave at home and out in the world. Many dog obedience instructors offer classes specifically geared toward helping dogs and their people practice for the CGC test. Ask your regular dog obedience instructor about this test, and whether she offers classes specifically to help dogs pass the test. Unlike many other AKC-related activities, your Beagle does not have to be registered, or even a purebred, to participate in the CGC program.

To pass the test and earn the CGC certificate, dogs successfully perform 10 activities.

Test 1: Accepting a Friendly Stranger This test demonstrates that the dog will allow a friendly stranger to approach and speak to the handler in a natural, everyday situation. The evaluator walks up to the dog and handler and greets the handler in a friendly manner, ignoring the dog.

The evaluator and handler shake hands and exchange pleasantries. The dog must show no sign of resentment or shyness, and must not break position or try to go to the evaluator.

Test 2: Sitting Politely for Petting This test demonstrates that the dog will allow a friendly stranger to touch him while he is out with his handler. With the dog sitting at the handler's side, to begin the exercise, the evaluator pets the dog on the head and body. The handler may talk to his or her dog throughout the exercise. The dog may stand in place as he is petted. The dog must not show shyness or resentment.

Test 3: Appearance and Grooming This practical test demonstrates that the dog will welcome being groomed and examined and will permit someone, such as a veterinarian, groomer or friend of the owner, to do so. It also demonstrates the owner's care, concern and sense of responsibility. The evaluator inspects the dog to determine if he is clean and groomed. The dog must appear to be in healthy condition (i.e., proper weight, clean, healthy and alert). The handler should supply the comb or brush commonly used on the dog. The evaluator then softly combs or brushes the dog, and in a natural manner, lightly examines the ears and gently picks up each front foot. It is not necessary for the dog to hold a specific position during the examination, and the handler may talk to the dog, praise him and give encouragement throughout.

Test 4: Out for a Walk (Walking on a Loose Lead) This test demonstrates that the handler is in control of the dog. The dog may be on either side of the handler. The dog's position should leave no doubt that the dog is attentive to the handler and is responding to the handler's movements and changes of direction. The dog need not be perfectly aligned with the handler and need not sit when the handler stops. The evaluator may use a pre-plotted course or may direct the handler/dog team by issuing instructions or commands. In either case, there should be a right turn, left turn, and an about turn with at least one stop in between and another at the end. The handler may talk to the dog along the way, praise the dog, or give commands in a normal tone of voice. The handler may sit the dog at the halts if desired.

Test 5: Walking Through a Crowd This test demonstrates that the dog can move about politely in pedestrian traffic and is under control in public places. The dog and handler walk around and pass close to several people (at least three). The dog may show some interest in the strangers but should continue to walk with the handler, without evidence of over-exuberance, shyness, or resentment. The handler may talk to the dog and encourage or praise the dog throughout the test. The dog should not jump on people in the crowd or strain on the leash.

Test 6: *Sit* and *Down* on Command and Staying in Place This test demonstrates that the dog has training, will respond to the handler's commands to *sit* and *down* and will remain in the place commanded by the handler (*sit* or *down* position, whichever the handler prefers). The dog must do *sit* and *down* on command, then the owner chooses the position for leaving the dog in the *stay*. Prior to this test, the dog's leash is replaced with a line 20 feet long. The handler may take a reasonable amount of time and use more than one command to get the dog to *sit* and then *down*. The evaluator must determine if the dog has responded to the handler's commands. The handler may not force the dog into position but may touch the dog to offer gentle guidance. When instructed by the evaluator, the handler tells the dog to stay and walks forward the length of the line, turns and returns to the dog at a natural pace. The dog must remain in the place in which it was left (it may change position) until the evaluator instructs the handler to release the dog. The dog may be released from the front or the side.

Test 7: Coming When Called This test demonstrates that the dog will come when called by the handler. The handler will walk ten feet from the dog, turn to face the dog, and call the dog. The handler may use encouragement to get the dog to come. Handlers may choose to tell dogs to "stay" or "wait" or they may simply walk away, giving no instructions to the dog.

Test 8: Reaction to Another Dog This test demonstrates that the dog can behave politely around other dogs. Two handlers and their dogs approach each other from a distance of about 20 feet, stop, shake hands and exchange pleasantries, and continue on for about 10 feet. The dogs should show no more than casual interest in each other. Neither dog should go to the other dog or its handler.

Test 9: Reaction to Distraction This test demonstrates that the dog is confident at all times when faced with common distracting situations. The evaluator will select and present two distractions. Examples of distractions include dropping a chair, rolling a crate dolly past the dog, having a jogger run in front of the dog, or dropping a crutch or cane. The dog may express natural interest and curiosity and/or may appear slightly startled but should not panic, try to run away, show aggressiveness, or bark. The handler may talk to the dog and encourage or praise it throughout the exercise.

Test 10: Supervised Separation This test demonstrates that a dog can be left with a trusted person, if necessary, and will maintain training and good manners. Evaluators are encouraged to say something like, "Would you like me to watch your dog?" and then take hold of the dog's leash. The owner will go out of sight for three minutes. The dog does not have to stay in position but should not continually bark, whine, or pace unnecessarily, or show anything stronger than mild agitation or nervousness. Evaluators may talk to the dog but should not engage in excessive talking, petting, or management attempts (e.g, "There, there, it's alright").

Activities

If you and your Beagle have a knack for training, your Beagle has already passed basic obedience, and you want to go further, consider signing up for some advanced activities. When Beagles get enough exercise, interesting mental challenges, and plenty of time with their people, they reach their maximum potential. The activities you choose depend on your preferences and your Beagle's talents, but the following make use of the Beagle's natural instincts and special skills.

Tracking

This fun, outdoorsy activity is a natural for Beagles because of their highly developed scenting ability. Tracking tests how well a dog can follow the scent of a human. Really talented trackers sometimes end up working professionally as search-and-rescue dogs, but most people train their dogs for tracking competition just for fun, and for the prestige of earning tracking titles.

Helpful Hints

Dog training clubs all over the country offer specialized training classes for activities like tracking, conformation, rally and obedience, agility, hunting, and the Canine Good Citizen test.

Tracking tests are hosted by local clubs. Judges mark out tracks of varying difficulty for dogs to follow, and tracklayers walk the tracks, so the Beagles have a scent to follow. Dogs follow their designated track (one at a time) on a long leash, and you follow along. To pass the test, your Beagle must stay on the track as the tracklayer walked it,

and follow it to the end to retrieve an article (typically a glove) placed at the end of the track.

Dogs earn titles at each of three levels in tracking, if they successfully navigate the scent trail. Each successive title requires following a more complicated scent trail. Titles are Tracking Dog (TD), Tracking Dog Excellent (TDX), and Variable Surface Tracking (VST).

Any dog over six months old and registered with the American Kennel Club can participate in AKC tracking events.

Rally

Competitive obedience isn't every Beagle's favorite sport, but rally is a less rigorous and more relaxed, fun version of obedience that many Beagles really enjoy. You and your Beagle compete together over a course of stations. Each station requires that you and your Beagle perform a particular obedience command, as indicated on a sign. These are simple at basic levels, such as "stop and down," or more complicated at higher levels, such as "double left about turn" or going over jumps.

Dogs in rally compete at three levels: Novice, Advanced, and Excellent. They can earn titles as they progress through these levels. Rally titles are Rally Novice (RN), Rally Advanced (RA), Rally Excellent (RE), and Rally Advanced Excellent (RAE). To participate, Beagles must be registered with the AKC and be at least six months old.

Agility

This high-energy race gives each dog, accompanied by his handler, a chance to navigate a course of tunnels, A-frames, jumps, rings, weave poles, and other obstacles. The fastest dogs win. While some breeds like Border Collies and Shetland Sheepdogs will probably always dominate the sport, many Beagles think it's plenty of fun.

As dogs achieve successive levels of skill, they can earn agility titles. Agility trials are divided into three classes. Standard Class includes contact objects like the A-frame and see-saw. Jumpers with Weaves classes use only jumps, tunnels, and weave poles, with no contact objects. FAST (an acronym for Fifteen and Send Time) pushes dogs to achieve greater speed and accuracy. In each class, there are Novice, Open, Excellent, and Master titles. The highest possible title in agility is the MACH title, which stands for Master Agility Championship title. It's rare for a Beagle to obtain a MACH title, but it has happened. Maybe your high-speed Beagle will be next.

To complete in AKC agility events, dogs must be registered with the AKC, and be at least six months old.

Field Trials and Hunt Tests

Beagling is the sport of hunting rabbits with Beagles, and it is, of course, what Beagles were originally created to do. While most people no longer need to hunt rabbits for dinner, many still participate in the sport for fun. Watching a pair or whole pack of Beagles catch wind of a scent trail and start up their beautiful baying music is an amazing experience.

Competing with a Beagle in Beagling events takes some knowledge. There are many different kinds of Beagle field trials that operate in different ways. Each has its own protocol, terminology, and traditions, from wearing the right costumes to the calling out of "Tally-ho!" when someone spots the rabbit or hare. You have to see it and experience it to really get the feel for how it all works. Fortunately, Beaglers are typically a friendly bunch, happy to bring more interested people and their hounds into the fold.

Breed Truths

If you want a Beagle primarily for hunting and/or field trials, you will need to raise and train your Beagle for that purpose. Even though your Beagle will still be a pet, training a hunting dog is a specialized field. Find a Beagle from a breeder who breeds for this purpose, so your Beagle will be most likely to have the knack for hunting. Then, ask a lot of questions. Get involved with the Beagling community and you'll learn a lot. Also, find books about training hunting Beagles. An in-depth treatment of training the hunting Beagle is beyond the scope of this book, but there are other books particularly devoted to this subject, such as *Beagle Basics: Training of the Hunting Beagle* by Bill Bennett.

Both the American Kennel Club and the United Kennel Club hold Beagling events. AKC Beagle field trials and hunt tests are divided into several categories.

- **Brace trials** are the original type of Beagle field trial. Two or three Beagles run together and must accurately follow the trail of a rabbit. They don't catch the rabbit, and speed is not the object. In fact, Beagles move pretty slowly in a brace trial. The object is to precisely follow the scent trail.

- **Small Pack Option trials** run packs of seven Beagles. They must find the scent of a rabbit and chase it with enthusiasm, without losing the trail. They are judged on how well they follow the trail and stay together.
- **Large Pack trials** run packs of up to 25 dogs. They chase a hare instead of a rabbit, and must run for at least three hours, at the level where they can earn the first level of field trial title.
- **Gun Dog Brace trials** run pairs of Beagles, but they have to find their own rabbit and are judged on how well they search for and then follow the rabbit trail. This trial includes a gunshot, to judge whether the dogs are afraid of the sound of a gun (they should not be).
- **Hunt Tests for Two Couple Packs** are tests evaluating packs of four dogs that find their own rabbit and follow its trail. Each pack runs for at least 20 minutes and is also tested for gun shyness. Dogs who pass the hunt test earn the Master Hunter (MH) title.

Competing in field trials requires some experience, and it's a good idea to attend a few field trials and watch to get the feel for how it all works. Join a local field trial club and start training. Field trials can seem complicated to a beginner, but can also become addictive to those who really get into the sport.

The United Kennel Club also has an active Beagle Program, for Beagles registered with the UKC rather than the AKC. To find out more about the UKC Beagle Program, go to the UKC home page at *www.ukcdogs.com* and click on "Dog Events," then scroll down and click on "Hunting Programs."

Conformation Dog Shows

If you watched Uno win the Westminster Kennel Club dog show in 2007, you may have thought to yourself, "My Beagle could do that." Maybe you're right. Some people really enjoy competing in conformation shows with their purebred dogs.

To compete in conformation, your Beagle cannot be spayed or neutered. Conformation shows are for the purpose of evaluating breeding stock, and the dogs are judged according to the written breed

Fun Facts

The land where Beagling began may Beagle no more. In 2004, Beagling and fox hunting were banned in England and Wales with the adoption of the Hunting Act, which deemed these sports as cruel. Hunting with dogs was also banned in Scotland in 2002. Don't worry about cruelty in competitive Beagling in the United States, however. Rabbits and hare are flushed and chased, but not captured, in these events. The competition is based on how well the Beagles follow the scent trail, not on actually catching the prey animal itself.

standard for perfection in order to create more perfect dogs. Since most pets should be spayed or neutered to prevent unwanted puppies, dog shows aren't necessarily an appropriate hobby.

However, if you bought your Beagle with one eye on the show ring, and you have studied the breed standard and think you have a good prospect,

ACTIVITIES Junior Showmanship

If you have kids (or if you are a kid) and you like the idea of showing your Beagle in a dog show, consider getting involved in Junior Showmanship. This program teaches kids how to handle dogs in the show ring, and because Beagles are so agreeable, kid-friendly, and sized just right, many kids compete with them (although you'll see lots of other breeds, too). Unlike regular conformation shows, during which the dog is judged, Junior Showmanship judges the handlers. Junior Showmanship teaches good sportsmanship as well as the art of showing a dog in a dog show, and many kids get very involved. Junior Showmanship is open to kids ages 9 to 18.

Not quite ready for that level? Then check into your local 4-H club. Many 4-H programs also hold dog shows for kids, and any dog will do, including mixed breeds. For more information on Junior Showmanship, visit the AKC page for Juniors: www.akc.org/kids_juniors/index.cfm. For more information on 4-H, see www.4-h.org.

give it a try. There is much to learn, and a good breeder may also be willing to mentor you through the process. Visit some dog shows and talk to some of the exhibitors there to get a feel for what the life is like. You may never look back.

While a complete explanation of conformation showing is beyond the scope of this book, basically what is involved is that your Beagle will be judged, not against other Beagles in the ring, but against the written breed standard (you can read it in Chapter 1 of this book). Judges are specifically trained to judge Beagles by this standard. The dog in the ring who, in the judge's opinion, best fits the standard, wins.

There are three types of conformation shows for American Kennel Club-registered dogs. All-breed shows are shows that any AKC-recognized breed may enter. The Westminster Kennel Club dog show is this kind of show. Each breed is judged separately, and judges pick a Best of Breed for each breed. Then, the Best of Breeds all compete against other breeds in their group. For example, the best Beagle, the best Basset Hound, the best Greyhound, the best Bloodhound, and the best Rhodesian Ridgeback (all members of the Hound group) compete against each other for Best of Group. When Uno won the Westminster Kennel Club dog show, he first had to win as the best Beagle. Then, he won as the best Hound. That one best hound, whichever breed it is, goes on to compete against the best Sporting Dog, the best Working Dog, the best Terrier, the best Non-Sporting Dog, the best Toy Dog, and the best Herding Dog. These seven dogs are judged by a best-in-show-qualified judge. The winner receives the much-coveted Best in Show award—the best dog in the entire show. That's what Uno won, and that's why it was such a big deal.

The other types of shows are Specialty shows, in which the entire show is limited to one breed, and Group shows, in which the entire show is limited to one group. The National Beagle Club has a Specialty show every year, and only Beagles are allowed. A Group show could be all Hounds, or all Terriers, or all Sporting Dogs, or any of the other groups.

To compete in any of these shows, dogs must be individually registered with the American Kennel Club (or the United Kennel Club, for UKC shows). They must be six months of age or older, be of the correct breed, and meet all eligibility requirements, as stated in that breed's breed standard. For example, a Beagle over 15 inches would be disqualified.

How dogs are divided and judged depends on the show. Males and females are sometimes judged separately, and so are dogs of different classes. Classes include Puppy, for dogs between six and 12 months; Twelve-to-Eighteen Months, for dogs that are of that age but not yet champions; Novice, for dogs six months or older that haven't achieved certain wins yet; Amateur-Owner-Handler, for dogs that are not champions and are handled by their owners instead of professional handlers; Bred by Exhibitor, for dogs that are exhibited by their owner-breeders and are not yet champions; American-Bred, for dogs born in the U.S. that are not yet champions; and Open, for any dogs that are at least six months.

During the show, the dogs (whether all Beagles, all Hounds, or all Best of Group winners, or as appropriate for the particular class being judged) line up outside the ring, then at the signal, the dogs and their handlers move into the ring and walk or run in a circle. The judge will then tell you what to do. Sometimes he will look at all the dogs as they stand still, or watch them run. Then he will look at each one, examining it on a table and feeling it to be sure it has the right body type and no problems, such as crooked limbs, a kinked tail, or undescended testicles. Then he will watch each dog (with handler) run away from him, and towards him, so he can watch and assess the dog's movement. Finally, the judge will make a decision, and point to the winner and the runners-up, which include such distinctions as Best of Breed (the best dog in that breed), Best of Winners (the dog judged as the best between the best male and best female, called Winners Dog and Winners Bitch), and the Best of Opposite Sex (the best dog that is the opposite sex of the Best of Breed winner).

If you are new to dog shows, the whole process can seem pretty intimidating. Are you doing the right thing? Are you acting the right way? Are you breaking any rules? More experienced handlers sometimes get annoyed with newbies, but others are very helpful and encouraging. If you and your Beagle really enjoy showing, then keep doing it. Dog shows are pretty competitive but they can also become a lifestyle. A lot of people spend almost every single weekend on the road with their dogs, competing in conformation shows. The more you do it, the more confident you will get, and the better you will get. If your dog really is made for the show ring, you can probably eventually put a title on him. When he gets a sufficient number of wins, he will earn the title of Champion, which means you can put a CH before his name. Now that's prestige.

To learn even more about conformation showing and how to get involved in dog shows with your purebred registered Beagle, check out the popular book *Show Me!* by my friend and colleague, Caroline Coile, Ph.D.

Pet Therapy Work

Therapy dogs visit hospitals, nursing homes, and anywhere else where people can benefit from petting a good dog. Beagles make excellent therapy dogs because they are laid-back, friendly, small enough not to intimidate people, and easily recognizable. They also enjoy spending time with you as you travel to different places, visiting people who need canine therapy, whether that is a children's hospital, senior center, veteran's home, or a school where children practice reading to dogs. (Westminster winner Uno is a certified therapy dog.)

But not just any dog can trot into a hospital and jump on the beds. Most facilities require dogs to be certified, which typically requires that dogs have the Canine Good Citizen certificate.

Keep your Beagle busy and you'll both be better for it. An active, physically-fit Beagle who has plenty to think about, decisions to make, and the chance to work hard with you at his side, will be a fulfilled, happy, and better-behaved pet. Beagles are one of the most versatile breeds, so no matter what you want to do with them—agility, tracking, conformation, therapy—if you are dedicated to the task, you will likely succeed. Assess your Beagle's individual talent, then go for it.

Leash Training

1 Put a collar around your Beagle's neck and attach a leash. Let your Beagle get used to the feel of it. (Don't leave him unsupervised with the leash attached!)

2 Pick up the leash and follow your Beagle around wherever he wants to go, so he gets used to the idea of you on the other end of the leash.

3 Now, the lure. Show your Beagle a small treat, and coax him to follow you. As soon as he moves with you for a few steps, say "walk," then praise him and give him the treat. If he doesn't move with you, do not reward him, but work on gaining his interest with the treat. Keep working (and producing new treats) until he willingly follows you. Never pull or jerk on the leash.

4 Within a day or two your Beagle should begin to follow along with you. Move your practice outside and keep working. If you keep your Beagle focused on you and the treats you have in your pocket, he will be less likely to pull. When he gets older, if he does start pulling, always stop and wait for him to come back to you before moving ahead. He'll soon learn that he only gets to go forward when he doesn't pull on the leash.

The *Sit* Command

1 Beagles love treats, so the best way to teach *sit* is to lure your puppy into a sitting position, using a treat as the lure. Begin by getting a small treat and placing your Beagle in front of you.

2 Hold the treat just about your Beagle's nose, then gradually move it back over the top of his head. As he looks up to follow the treat, he will probably sit naturally. As he does this, say, "Sit," then give him the treat and praise him.

3 If your Beagle doesn't naturally sit, bring the treat back in front of him, then slowly pull it back again, but gently lower his rear end into a sitting position as you do it. Say "Sit!" as you do this, then give him the treat and praise him.

4 If your Beagle stands, do it a few more times. If he stays sitting, prop his rear end back up again. Most puppies will only practice two or three times at first, but repeating this practice several times a day for several days will quickly teach your Beagle the meaning of the command *sit*.

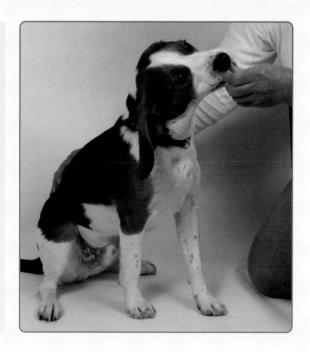

The *Stay* Command

1 Begin by having your Beagle sit (with his collar and leash on), using the treat lure, or just using the command, if he has already mastered it.

2 Hold up your palm at your Beagle's eye level, and say, "Stay." Wait for just a few seconds. If he stays sitting, give him a treat and praise him. If he makes any move to stand up, have him sit again, then try it again.

3 Keep practicing this part. Be sure to offer a treat before your Beagle stands up or moves toward you, even if you wait only two seconds. It may take a few tries for your Beagle to understand that *stay* means don't move, but when treats are involved, he'll quickly figure it out.

4 Once he begins to understand what you want, gradually increase the time before offering the treat. After your Beagle stays for about five seconds, start stepping back after you give the cue. Always come back to your Beagle to release him and give him the treat. If you release him and have him come to you, he will confuse stay with *come*.

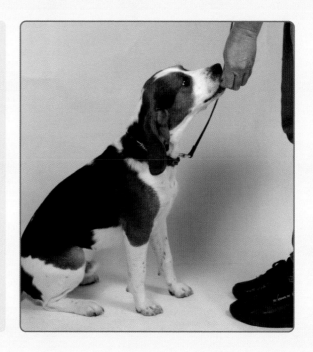

Chapter Eight

Grooming a Beagle

V isit a dog show and you will see a lot of primping going on backstage. Poodles, Maltese, Sheepdogs, Shih Tzu, and Yorkshire Terriers get washed and combed, blowdried and beribboned, but the Beagles just get a good wash, a quick brush-up on the undersides of their tails, and jump into the ring. No muss, no fuss.

One of the Beagle's stellar qualities is how easy he is to groom. You don't have to pay a professional groomer every month. Everything your Beagle needs, you can provide quickly and easily at home. But that doesn't mean you don't have to brush your Beagle. Grooming is an important part of maintaining your Beagle's health and keeping an eye on how he develops. Grooming stimulates your Beagle's skin, keeps his coat healthy and shiny, and minimizes shed hair in the house. Grooming keeps nails short, teeth clean, and fleas at bay. It also gives you and your Beagle the chance to enjoy some relaxed one-on-one time.

To be a good groomer to your Beagle, don't neglect any of the important grooming chores. Instead, make them a part of your regular routine and watch your Beagle sparkle.

Beagle Grooming Basics

Don't worry about fancy grooming tools or time-consuming detangling, but do make regular time for grooming. Ideally, you should spend about five minutes every day grooming your Beagle, just so it becomes a regular part of your Beagle's day. A daily once-over is the best way to make sure everything is okay. You'll see less Beagle hair in the house and on your clothes, and your Beagle will quickly come to enjoy the routine, whether you groom in the morning after you groom yourself, or use grooming as a nice way to wind down at the end of the day. If a daily grooming session just isn't feasible for you, aim for at least once a week.

What you do during each grooming session will vary, depending on how often each chore needs to be done. The schedule (on page 124) works well for most Beagles, but you may want to adapt it to fit your life. This is just

HOME BASICS
Beagle Grooming Schedule

Daily	Weekly	Monthly
Once-over	Trim tips of nails	Bathe/shampoo
Brush coat	Clean ears	Apply pest control
Brush teeth (ideal)	Brush teeth (if you can't do it daily)	
Wash face		

a guideline: Four things to do each day, three things to do each week, and two things to do each month. Descriptions of how to do each of the grooming items mentioned follow.

The Once-over

Once a day, give your Beagle a once-over. Check your Beagle with your eyes and hands to make sure everything looks normal, similar to what your veterinarian does at a check-up. If you do this every day, your Beagle will accept the once-over as just another part of life in a human world.

This check is very important for your Beagle's health. If you never look at the insides of your Beagle's ears or his rear end, if you never feel his skin,

CHECKLIST

Grooming Supplies

Keep all these Beagle grooming supplies in one place, such as in a tote, shower caddy, or basket, and you'll always have everything you need at hand.

- ✔ Natural bristle brush, hound glove, or rubber curry comb
- ✔ Toothbrush and toothpaste formulated for dogs
- ✔ Nail trimmer for small-to-medium-sized dogs (depending on your Beagle's size)
- ✔ Styptic powder (such as Kwik-Stop) in case of bleeding during nail trimming
- ✔ Ear wash and cotton balls
- ✔ Gentle shampoo formulated for dogs
- ✔ Spot-on flea control product

how will you know if something changes? A daily once-over gives you a baseline idea of what is normal for your Beagle. If you ever do notice any changes—such as a lump or rash or swelling or anything else—you can alert your veterinarian and catch any developing health issues as soon as possible.

The once-over is also a great way to prepare for a grooming session, both mentally and physically. Your Beagle will know just what to expect when you start checking out his ears and eyes and rubbing his skin.

Breed Needs

If your Beagle's tear stains continue despite a daily wipe-down, or your Beagle has red, runny, or otherwise irritated eyes, see your veterinarian. Your Beagle may need medication for a tear duct disorder.

1. Move your hands all over your Beagle, rubbing his skin to loosen shed hair and stimulate oil production, as if you were giving him a massage.
2. While you are doing this, feel for any lumps or bumps, rough patches, or other skin changes.
3. Look at your Beagle's eyes. Are they shiny and clear?
4. Look at his nose. Is it running?
5. Check his teeth by lifting up his lips. Do they look clean and white?
6. Lift up each ear. How does it look in there? Clean or dirty? Rub his ears and the top of his head.
7. Feel the loose skin around his neck.
8. Look at and rub his belly.
9. Peek under the tail to be sure everything looks clean and normal.
10. Pick up each paw, one at a time, and press gently on the paw pads. Wiggle each nail.
11. Praise your Beagle!
12. If you see anything strange or abnormal, alert your veterinarian.

Brushing

Beagles love to be brushed, and you'll love the effects, which include a softer, shinier coat and less shed hair. Beagles can shed a lot, especially during seasonal transitions, but daily brushing will make a big difference in how much you notice it.

No need to buy any fancy brushes or combs. Beagles need only a natural bristle brush, hound glove, or rubber curry comb. A hound glove fits over your hand and has rubber nubs on the palm. Rub it over your Beagle's coat and shed hair falls away. A curry comb looks like a hard rubber scrub brush. Both are ideal for the Beagles' short, hard coat, but a regular bristle brush works just fine, too.

Brush your Beagle from head to tail with firm but gentle strokes. Most people prefer to brush their Beagles outside so the flying hair stays out of the house. Needless to say, don't brush your Beagle while wearing your nice black dress or the suit you plan to wear to work.

If your Beagle's face always looks clean and shiny, you don't really have to wipe it down, but some dogs enjoy this refreshing part of grooming. If your Beagle tends to have weepy eyes and tear stains, a daily face-washing becomes even more important for good looks as well as good health. Runny eyes can result in bacterial infections because the moist under-eye area attracts bacteria. A daily gentle wipe-down under the eyes can keep tear stains at bay and keep the under-eye area drier.

Dental Care

You brush your teeth every day to prevent tooth decay, and your Beagle needs daily dental care, too. Dogs suffer from many of the same dental problems humans do, including infections that can enter the bloodstream and affect the major organ systems. Many veterinary dentists agree that poor dental health could result in serious health problems and even early death. At the very least, regular brushing will reduce the need

Helpful Hints

When dogs eat kibble, the food naturally scrapes off the inner sides of the teeth, so you only need to focus on the outer surfaces you can see when brushing your Beagle's teeth.

for expensive dental cleanings as your Beagle ages. Brushing is a very important part of keeping your Beagle healthy.

Any soft toothbrush will work, but brushes made for dogs have longer handles, which can make it easier to reach back teeth. Don't use a toothpaste made for humans. Dogs shouldn't swallow these, and you can't exactly tell your Beagle to spit. Instead, purchase a toothpaste specifically made for dogs. These pastes are flavored with doggy-delicious flavors like chicken or liver, so your Beagle will probably enjoy them.

How to Brush Your Beagle's Teeth

Despite how often you explain to your Beagle the importance of good dental hygiene, a few Beagles are simply very resistant to having their teeth brushed. For these tough cases, you have a few options. Wrap a piece of

gauze around your finger and rub down the outsides of your Beagle's teeth as often as you can—at least weekly. Offer your Beagle dental treats approved by the Veterinary Oral Health Council. You can also buy dental sprays and washes, or even tooth-washing enzyme-based products you can add to your dog's water. Although brushing is best, these other options are better than no dental care at all, and can also be good adjuncts to brushing. Now, for the brushing:

1. Get your Beagle used to having you put things in his mouth. If you have been doing the daily once-over, your Beagle may not mind one bit if you start brushing his teeth. If yours is a little shy, however, begin by letting him lick some of the toothpaste off your finger. Touch his teeth and praise him. Let him sniff the toothbrush, then let him lick some paste off the brush.

2. When your Beagle is comfortable with the toothbrush, you can start brushing. Do just a few seconds at a time for puppies, so they don't get bored or start to dislike brushing. Work up to more thorough brushing as your Beagle gets older and used to the process.

3. To brush, begin at the front. Lift up your Beagle's lips and gently brush the outsides of his front teeth in a circular motion. That's usually enough for the first few times.

4. As your Beagle gets more comfortable with brushing, take a little more time and work the brush around to the sides. Be sure to get to all the back teeth, brushing both upper and lower sets.

5. Always talk cheerfully to your Beagle as you brush, and praise him lavishly. If your Beagle misbehaves or resists, don't scold him. Stop and try again later. You don't want him to associate any negative experiences with brushing.

6. End each brushing session with a dental-friendly treat.

Breed Needs

Daily tooth brushing can make a big difference in your dog's veterinary dental needs. Some well-brushed dogs never need an expensive professional dental cleaning. However, even with regular brushing, a few individual dogs still tend to accumulate a lot of plaque on their teeth, which can lead to tooth decay and other serious dental and health problems. Your veterinarian should check your dog's teeth every year. If necessary, your dog may need a professional cleaning under a general anesthesia, especially as he gets older. Don't neglect this important aspect of your Beagle's veterinary care.

Nail Care

Natural diggers, Beagles tend to have big paws and strong nails that grow quickly. Even with regular walks, most Beagles need a nail trim every week or two, but trimming a Beagle's nails can be difficult if your Beagle isn't used to it. The trick to nail trimming is to start early and trim often.

If you begin by trimming your puppy's nails the first week you bring him home, he might object, but he won't object for long. Beagles typically accept anything that becomes part of their routine, so making nail trimming part of the routine *right away* will make a huge difference in how much effort it takes to trim your Beagle's nails for the rest of his life. Even if your puppy's nails don't need trimming, touch each nail with the trimmer at least once a week. Or, start out doing just one nail a week.

As your Beagle gets older and nails grow faster and stronger, nail trimming will become even more important. Untrimmed nails can be painful to walk on and can even spread out foot pads so your dog can't walk normally.

Keep them short so they don't tap the floor as your Beagle walks, and your Beagle will be more sure-footed and pain-free.

Trimming the nail isn't difficult, but it does require some specific knowledge. First of all, you want to cut the nail without cutting the quick. As your Beagle's nail grows, so does the *quick*—a vein inside the nail that can bleed if you accidentally snip it. Snipping the quick hurts, and can cause dogs to fear future nail clipping events, so try to avoid it. If it happens, however, your Beagle will recover. A little styptic powder (such as Kwik-Stop) will staunch the bleeding. If you don't have any around, the bleeding will stop on its own after awhile.

The less often you trim nails, the longer the quick grows. Nails trimmed frequently—preferably once each week—encourage the quick to withdraw farther back into the nail, making quick-clipping accidents less likely.

In light-colored nails, you can often see how far the quick extends, but in dark nails, you have to guess. If you just clip off the very tips of your Beagle's nails once a week, however, you will almost certainly avoid the quick.

Use a nail trimmer made for dogs. It doesn't matter what kind you use. Some look more like little curved hedge trimmers, and some are guillotine style. The nail goes inside a small metal oval, then you squeeze. Whichever style is more comfortable for you is fine, but the blade should be sharp to make a clean cut. Position the trimmer over the tip of the nail, so you cut off just a few millimeters of nail. Hold the paw gently, then quickly squeeze to clip off the end. File rough edges with a metal nail file so they don't scratch you.

Helpful Hints

Some people prefer to use a nail grinder or dremel-tool-style trimmer instead of a clipper to keep their Beagle's nails short. These tools work well if used correctly. Grinders allow you to grind down, smooth, and shape the nail all in one step, using this electric tool. However, the grinder moves quickly and can generate a lot of heat. Just be careful not to grind off too much nail, or accidentally grind your dog's skin. Use it just a few seconds at a time, so the nail doesn't overheat.

Ear Care

Any dog with long floppy ears is at risk for ear infections because dirt and moisture can get trapped under the ear flaps, attracting bacteria and yeast. Your Beagle may never have any problems with his ears, but keep an eye on them anyway, just to be sure. Signs of an ear infection include ear scratching and head shaking, plus more obvious signs such as redness inside the ears.

To keep your Beagle's ears clean and dry, you can wipe them out when you are washing your Beagle's face. Just wipe out the parts you can see. Or, to be really

thorough, use a canine ear wash you can buy at a pet store. Ear washes dissolve wax and flush out bacteria to keep ears healthy and clean. Use the ear wash according to the package directions.

Bathing

Beagles tend to be pretty clean animals and stay looking good with regular brushing, but a monthly bath with a gentle, skin-soothing shampoo formulated for pets will keep your Beagle smelling sweet and will help remove even more shed hair.

Helpful Hints

Try to keep your Beagle inside after a bath, until he is completely dry. Wet Beagles tend to like to dry themselves by rolling around in the dirt!

131

As with any other aspect of grooming, get your Beagle used to bathing at an early age, so he accepts it as part of his normal life. Because the Beagle has a short coat, bathing won't take long, but select your shampoo carefully. Beagles tend to have sensitive skin. Shampoos with chemical sudsing agents can be harsh and irritating. Gentle, hypo-allergenic shampoos formulated especially for dogs (don't use your shampoo, it's the wrong pH balance) can actually help improve skin quality, rather than stripping it of its essential natural oils. Shampoos with natural botanicals and organic ingredients may also be particularly gentle. If your Beagle already has any skin issues or flea issues, your veterinarian may recommend a specific shampoo.

Bathe your Beagle in the bathtub, or outside with the hose, if that's easier. Just be sure to test the hose water first, to be sure the sun hasn't heated it to scalding temperatures. Grab your grooming supplies, and follow these steps for a squeaky-clean Beagle.

1. Put on your Beagle's leash and collar so you can hold on to him. You don't need a sudsy Beagle racing through the house. Put him in the tub or in a child's swimming pool in the yard.
2. Turn on the water and test it to be sure it is lukewarm or cool. Using a large plastic cup or hose attachment, thoroughly wet your Beagle's coat. Add a small amount of gentle shampoo and work it into your Beagle's coat. Don't forget the belly, legs, under the tail, and the tops of the ears.
3. Be careful not to get soap inside your Beagle's ears or eyes. If you are worried, you can plug your Beagle's ears with cotton balls and put a dab of petroleum jelly in the corner of each eye. Or, just keep soap away from these areas.
4. Rinse thoroughly, then rinse again. Even the Beagle's short coat can hold on to shampoo residue, which will attract dirt. Rinse longer than you think is necessary.
5. Towel dry your Beagle, and voila! He's clean.

Pest Control

Some Beagles never meet a flea or a tick, but most Beagles who spend a lot of time outside, especially in warmer areas of the country, are almost certainly going to encounter these horrible pests at some point in their lives. If you know fleas are a likely possibility where you live, preventing them is much easier than dealing with an infestation.

Helpful Hints

To keep fleas at bay and heal flea-bitten skin, look for shampoos containing Neem oil. This natural botanical ingredient comes from the fruits and seeds of the Neem evergreen tree, and naturally repels fleas. Neem oil is a great skin soother, too.

The best way to keep fleas and ticks off your Beagle is to use a veterinarian-prescribed monthly spot-on product like Frontline or Advantage. These products are generally recognized as safe when used correctly, and they really do work, killing pests on contact. Just put a few drops on your Beagle between his shoulder blades (follow package directions) once a month, after his bath, and you may never have a flea problem.

While grooming, always keep an eye out for signs of pests—actual fleas and ticks, or the little black specks that turn red when they get wet (that's flea dirt). Bathing can wash them away, but won't remove eggs and larvae from your home, so treat any signs of fleas immediately, and remove any pests you see immediately, too. A steel flea comb can help lift out fleas, or use your fingers. Drop fleas into a small cup of alcohol to kill them, then flush them away.

CAUTION

Ticks that stay attached to your Beagle for more than a few hours can transmit serious diseases including Lyme disease and Rocky Mountain Spotted Fever, so always remove a tick as soon as you find one. A burst tick can even infect you through the skin, so use caution and always use rubber gloves or a paper towel when handling ticks. Pull ticks straight out, at an angle perpendicular to the skin. Kill them by dropping them in a small cup of rubbing alcohol, then flush them down the toilet. If the site of a tick bite turns red or swells, consult your veterinarian.

If you suspect you have fleas in your home, take action immediately. Treat your pet, then immediately wash all pet bedding, and your own bedding if your Beagle sleeps with you. Vacuum the whole house and dispose of the vacuum bag outside. Repeat daily until the infestation is under control. Regular, old-fashioned bathing and vacuuming go a long way toward controlling a flea infestation.

Chapter Nine

Senior Beagles

Whether you've adopted a canine senior citizen or the Beagle you brought home as a puppy is finally reaching his golden years, eventually you will be faced with the changing needs of a senior Beagle. Some Beagles sail through old age smoothly, barely slowing down until they reach the end. Others have a bumpier road, but you can help smooth the way by being prepared.

Of course, the best way to help your Beagle age gracefully is by keeping him healthy throughout his life. If your Beagle stays slim and trim rather than roly-poly, he will have a much easier time aging. Excessive weight puts excessive strain on joints and internal organs, and that makes aging particularly rough, especially if your Beagle develops arthritis (as many senior pets do). A fit Beagle will age more easily, too, maintaining muscle mass and maximizing organ function.

Regular grooming will help you spot any age-related changes, from dry skin to cancer, and paying attention to your Beagle every day will also help you notice any behavioral changes that could indicate medical problems, including canine dementia. Add regular veterinary check-ups so a professional eye can also be looking out for the signs of decline, and your Beagle will have the best chance for a long and healthy life.

How Beagles Age

As your Beagle ages, you can expect a few things to change. These are totally normal and nothing to worry about, although you should stay attuned to them. Natural signs of aging include a slightly reduced speed and activity level and a more mature attitude (less goofy

Breed Truths

We all get old eventually, and nobody lasts forever. Sadly for humans, dogs have comparatively short life spans. The average Beagle lives about 12 to 14 years, and while some last longer, others leave us at an earlier age. Make the most of the years you get with your Beagle by knowing what to look for and what to do about it.

puppy playfulness, although that may still occur). Some Beagles get hard of hearing, or a little bit stiff from arthritis.

Drastic changes, although they may come with age, are not a natural part of aging and should not be ignored. Just because your dog is old doesn't mean he should have to suffer. Call your veterinarian if your Beagle starts to experience any of the following changes, age-related or not.

- Noticeable stiffness, limping, or inability to jump up or down from things that were once easy to negotiate, reluctance to climb stairs or run as before, or yelping or flinching from pain when touched. Not only could these symptoms signal a spinal disk rupture, but they could also signify painful arthritis, which can be treated with medication.
- Any lumps or bumps, rough patches, or other skin changes. Some skin changes may be completely benign, but others could signify any of several types of canine cancer, including skin cancer and mast cell tumor. Catch most cancers early, and they can be effectively treated in dogs.
- Signs of deafness or blindness.
- Sudden weight gain or loss, which could signal a thyroid or other health problem.
- Increased thirst, hunger, and urination, which could signal diabetes or a kidney problem.
- Confusion, disorientation, getting "stuck" in corners, or seeming not to recognize familiar people or things. These are signs of canine dementia, an Alzheimer's-like condition that occurs in dogs. Canine dementia probably can't be cured, but can be treated and symptoms can improve with treatment.

Changes in Routine

If your Beagle isn't showing any sign of aging, there is no need to change his routine. However, if he starts to slow down or experience other problems, consult your veterinarian, then consider tweaking your Beagle's schedule. Maybe walks can be a little shorter, meals a little lighter, grooming a little gentler. Maybe this is a good time to add more laid-back, hanging-out time together with less physical and emotional stress. Does your Beagle need a few more daily bathroom breaks? Do you need to incorporate medication into the routine?

If you do change the routine, make sure you make a new routine. Remember, dogs, and especially senior dogs, rely on routines for stability and a sense of safety. Seniors will age more comfortably and with less stress if they know what to expect every day.

Senior Diet

You've seen "senior diet" dog foods on the shelf. Does your Beagle need one? If everything is normal, then probably not. Older Beagles need the

same nutrition as younger Beagles. However, if your Beagle starts to slow down, he may need fewer calories. If your Beagle starts to gain weight, consider reducing portions, or switching to a food with a lower calorie density.

Don't reduce protein for senior Beagles, however. Adequate protein will help fight muscle wasting, keeping your senior Beagle strong. Some senior formulas have less protein, but this is not necessary unless your Beagle suffers from a kidney problem. In that case, your veterinarian may recommend reducing the protein content of your Beagle's food. Certainly take your veterinarian's advice.

Exercise
Some people think seniors should exercise even more, to combat muscle wasting. Think of those senior citizens at the gym, lifting weights to help fight aging joints and weight gain. If your Beagle wants to keep moving, then go for it. Even if your Beagle is arthritic, exercise can help reduce pain

and increase range of motion. Exercise will also combat the weight gain so many senior Beagles tend to develop when they slow down.

However, some older Beagles really are in pain and don't want to exercise so much. In that case, take it easy. Don't skip the daily walk, but slow down and don't go quite as far. Watch your Beagle for signs that he is too tired— excessive panting, stopping, reluctance to go out. Take it easy and follow your Beagle's lead. If you are unsure about how much to exercise your Beagle, ask your veterinarian for advice. A check-up can confirm whether or not your Beagle should be cutting back on his physical activity.

Dealing with the Diseases of Aging

Some diseases typically occur in the first few years of life. Others are much more common in older dogs. Know what to look for so you and your veterinarian can keep your Beagle feeling fine.

Arthritis

Many dogs and many humans suffer from arthritis in old age, just because the wear and tear of daily life eventually takes its toll on joints. When your Beagle moves more slowly and stiffly, chances are he's got arthritis. The good news is that veterinarians have many treatments for this common condition.

Some people swear by glucosamine, a supplement usually derived from shellfish. Available in pills or powder to sprinkle on food, glucosamine has been shown to improve symptoms of arthritis in both pets and people. It's harmless and usually has no side effects, so it's worth a try. Ask your veterinarian about it. You can use glucosamine in conjunction with other treatments.

Dogs can also take non-steroidal anti-inflammatory medication

Breed Needs

Throughout your Beagle's life, it's a great idea to visit the veterinarian once a year, to make sure everything is going well and to get any necessary booster vaccinations. Once your Beagle begins to hit the golden years, however, most veterinarians recommend upping that annual check to twice yearly. Senior dogs can develop diseases and other health conditions more quickly than younger dogs, and those problems can progress faster. A check-up every six months starting at age 7 or 8 will help your veterinarian catch problems early.

(NSAIDs), just like humans do. While you might take Advil or Aleve for your achy joints, don't give those to your Beagle. Your veterinarian can prescribe a similar but animal-specific medication. However, be aware that these medications, although very effective for pain relief, can have serious side effects, from vomiting to kidney failure, especially after long-term use. Talk to your vet about the benefits and risks of NSAIDs for your arthritic Beagle.

Remember to keep providing your Beagle with gentle daily exercise, too. Moderate exercise does help arthritic pets feel better, as long as your veterinarian gives the okay.

Cancer

More and more pets suffer from cancer these days. Some people believe commercial pet food or a polluted environment are to blame. Others insist that dogs are living longer because of better vet care, so they are more likely to reach the age where cancer would develop. Either way, keep an eye out for lumps on your dog, changes in appetite or weight, unusual fatigue, or behavioral changes. Cancer can come in many forms with many symptoms, but only your veterinarian can diagnose it for sure. Just keep it on your radar as a possibility, especially if it encourages you not to miss your senior Beagle's regular, twice-yearly veterinary visit.

Diabetes

Any dog can develop diabetes, especially overweight seniors. Signs are excessive thirst and increased urination. Sometimes, dogs lose weight even though they are eating more. As with humans, diabetic dogs will require insulin injections to manage this serious disease. Your Beagle will have a much lower chance of becoming diabetic if you don't ever let him get overweight.

Hearing and Vision Loss

If your Beagle seems deafer than usual (actually not hearing you, as opposed to just ignoring you), or if he begins to bump into things or has trouble seeing in dim light, suspect hearing or vision loss. Make an appointment with your veterinarian to determine whether you are correct. Deaf or blind (or both!) senior Beagles can be difficult to manage because they are easily startled and can become anxious and snappy. However, if you are patient, you can help ease this difficult time for your Beagle. Routine is particularly essential for dogs with hearing or vision loss. Never sneak up on a deaf dog. Make a movement in front of him before touching him. For blind dogs, don't move the furniture around, and keep all pathways clear, so he can make his way around the house and yard without getting injured.

Breed Truths

Beagles tend to be particularly stoic dogs. They are so good at working hard without distraction and doing what it takes to get any job done that they tend to ignore their own discomfort. You may have to look particularly hard at your dog to recognize signs of pain or illness. If you aren't sure, talk to your veterinarian, just in case. Changes in behavior, movement, or skin may all signal a health problem.

Progressive Retinal Atrophy, Glaucoma, and Cataracts

Although Beagles tend to develop early-onset forms of these three common eye diseases, they all can develop in older dogs, too. Progressive Retinal Atrophy is a genetic defect that causes vision to deteriorate gradually, eventually resulting in blindness or near-blindness. Dogs tend to lose their central vision first and may be able to see via their peripheral vision into old age. This disease can't be treated, but it can be prevented through a genetic test in dogs. When dogs have the gene for this disease, they should not be bred. Glaucoma is a disease in which fluid builds up inside the eyeball, increasing pressure and eventually damaging the eye. Glaucoma is painful and often results in blindness. Cataracts are a condition in which the lens of the eye becomes opaque, obscuring vision. Some cataracts can be treated with surgery, depending on many factors, including the age and health of the dog.

Canine Dementia

This heartbreaking condition causes dogs to become senile. Some medications and dietary changes have been shown to improve symptoms. If your dog seems confused, disoriented, lost, or doesn't seem to recognize familiar people, talk to your veterinarian about the possibility that your Beagle has this problem, and ask what you can do about it.

Helping Senior Dogs Cope

Nobody likes getting old, and Beagles can get very frustrated when they can't do the things they used to do. Living with a senior Beagle can be frustrating for you, too. Where is your cheerful, healthy, active pet? Just remember that your Beagle gave you years of love and happiness. Now it's your turn to return the favor. People that work in animal shelters or volunteer for pet rescue groups often tell stories about families who had a dog for eight, ten, twelve years, then took it to the shelter when it became old and cranky or needed medical care. These dogs lose the only home they ever knew, just when they need stability the most.

Instead of giving up on your senior, please be patient and take the small amount of extra time it takes to give your aging Beagle extra attention, care, and understanding. Senior dogs can be exceptionally rewarding companions in a slower, softer, more laid-back way than a younger dog. You have a busy life, but your Beagle needs you now more than ever. This is the time to slow down and treasure the end of your Beagle's life, just as much if not more than you treasured his puppyhood.

Helpful Hints

Sometimes, other pet owners who have been through the experience of losing a pet can offer advice. Some say they just knew, when they looked in their pets' eyes, that it was time. They felt as if their dogs were telling them they were ready to go. Others felt they made the decision too soon and their pets weren't ready yet. They regretted rushing into the choice. But sometimes, other people can make you feel guilty about your decision or tell you what to do, when only you can make the decision for your own pet. Talk to people if you feel you need the support, or don't if you don't need the added pressure.

Saying Good-bye

When a pet becomes terminally ill, pet owners often struggle with a terrible question: Is it time to end my pet's life?

We cannot legally make this decision for our human family members, but we can make it for our pets. This is a mixed blessing. We have the power to relieve a pet of intense suffering. But how do we know if it's the right thing to do? How do we know when our pets are ready to go?

Nobody can answer this question for you—not even your veterinarian. If your pet is sick and suffering and no treatment relieves that suffering, or you believe the treatment will cause even more unnecessary suffering, you will have to decide for yourself whether it is time to let go or not.

For some people, euthanasia is the immediate best answer to end suffering. They would never put a pet through long painful medical procedures or let them suffer and die naturally, believing this is cruel and unnecessary. Others would never make the euthanasia choice, choosing instead to let a pet die naturally without interference other than pain control.

For most people, however, the answer lies somewhere in the middle. Your own moral compass will have to guide you on this one, but stay attuned to your pet, too. You are closer to your Beagle than anyone else, including your veterinarian, so you probably have the best idea about how much he is suffering. Does he still have that never-say-die spirit about him? That fire in his eyes? Or has he given up? Does he want release?

If the prognosis is grim, should you choose palliative care, or euthanasia?

Palliative Care

Palliative care means treating your Beagle's symptoms but letting him die naturally when the time comes. As veterinary medicine becomes better and better at pain management, more people are choosing this option. If you can keep your Beagle comfortable in his last days, minimizing suffering, then you can let him pass away when it happens naturally. Many people tell stories about choosing palliative care for their dogs, then spending the last days together and being there as their dogs finally passed. This can be an emotionally painful and drawn-out process, but many pet owners wouldn't have changed how they managed their pet's last days. Talk to your veterinarian about this option and what he can do to help ease your Beagle's suffering.

Euthanasia

Euthanasia means having a veterinarian administer an injection that ends your pet's life. Many people choose this option when they believe their pets are suffering more than necessary and they don't feel they can do anything to improve the situation. Many people tell stories about choosing euthanasia for their dogs, then being with them as they passed, holding them and watching their suffering disappear. Euthanasia is tough to handle for any pet owner, and even for veterinarians, who sometimes end up weeping with their long-time clients over the dogs they have treated for years. If you can be with your Beagle during this painful but important time, you can help ease his passing and assure him that you are there until the end. Consider it your final, last act of kindness to your faithful friend.

Helpful Hints

People who choose euthanasia for their pets often feel great peace that they made the right decision, just as many pet owners feel peace about their decision to choose palliative care. Let your conscience be your guide, and then let yourself be at peace with your decision, whatever it is. You've spent your Beagle's life doing your very best to make decisions that you believed were best for your Beagle. Do that to the end, and you'll be doing the right thing.

FYI: Seeking Comfort

Grief support hotlines, "virtual" pet memorials, forums where people can share their stories and feelings about pet loss, and special resources for children dealing with pet loss all can help you and your family deal with the loss of your Beagle. Some of the services also offer memorial products, such as headstones and urns.

- Association for Pet Loss and Bereavement, *www.aplb.org*
- Pet Loss Support Page, *www.pet-loss.net*
- Pet Loss Grief Support web site, *www.petloss.com*
- Rainbows Bridge *www.rainbowsbridge.com*

Grief Support

When you lose your Beagle, you will feel sad. You might even feel intense grief and think you'll never get over the loss. People often feel embarrassed to admit the depth of their grief over the death of a pet, but this is totally normal, especially these days, when pets have become such an important part of human families. We are intensely emotionally connected to our pets. How could we not feel pain when we lose them?

If you are having trouble dealing with the loss of your pet, give yourself some time. Let yourself grieve. If it helps, create a memorial to your pet. Write about him, or talk to your friends about him. Many people seek professional counseling to help them deal with pet loss, so don't feel silly seeking out the help you need.

Moving On

Living with a senior can be an intensely rewarding experience that turns heart-wrenching after your Beagle is finally gone. You are still here, however. You may need some time before you can even think about feeling normal again, and that's just fine. But when you do start to feel better and remember all the wonderful times you and your Beagle shared, remind yourself that your life is richer because you had a Beagle in it.

And maybe, just maybe, somewhere out there, another little Beagle puppy, or even a homeless senior Beagle, is looking for a home with a wonderful and experienced owner like you. If you have more to give to another lucky Beagle, and decide to share your life again, expect the next go-around to be similar, but also different. Every Beagle is an individual, and after living with a senior, you may have forgotten what it's like to deal with a younger dog again. No worries—just turn back to Chapter One and start this book . . . and your life . . . again.

Resources

Kennel & Breed Clubs

National Beagle Club of America
1075 Route 82, Suite 10
Hopewell, NJ 12533
http://clubs.akc.org/NBC

American Kennel Club
8051 Arco Corporate Drive, Suite 100
Raleigh, NC 27617-3390
(919) 233-9767
Office hours: 8:30 A.M.–5:00 P.M. (EST)
(Monday–Friday)
www.akc.org

United Kennel Club
100 E Kilgore Road
Kalamazoo MI 49002-5584
Office hours: 9:00 A.M.–4:30 P.M. (EST)
(Monday–Friday)
Phone: (269) 343-9020
Fax: (269) 343-7037
www.ukcdogs.com

Beagle Forums and On-line Discussion Groups
The Beagler Message Board Forum
americanbeagler.hunginboards.com

Beagle World
www.ourbeagleworld.com

Beagle Forums
www.beagleforums.com

Agility Beagles
pets.groups.yahoo.com/group/agilitybeagles/

Beagle Rescue
pets.groups.yahoo.com/group/BeagleRescue/

Periodicals

The American Beagler
www.americanbeagler.com

Better Beagling
www.betrbeagle.com

Show Beagle Quarterly
www.showbeaglequarterly.com

Small Pack Option Magazine
www.espomagazine.com

Health-related Associations and Foundations

American Veterinary Medical
  Society
www.avma.org

ASPCA Poison Control Center
888-426-4435

Orthopedic Foundation for Animals
(OFFA)
www.offa.org

Canine Eye Registration Foundation
(CERF)
www.vmdb.org

Dodgers List
www.dodgerslist.com.

American Holistic Veterinary
Medical Association
www.ahvma.org

Academy of Veterinary Homeopathy
www.theavh.org

Flower Essence Society
www.flowersociety.org

American Academy of Veterinary
Acupuncture
www.aava.org

American Veterinary Chiropractic
Association
www.animalchiropractic.org

International Association of Animal
Massage & Bodywork
www.iamb.org

National Animal Supplement
Council (NASC)
http://nasc.cc

Training and Activities

Association of Pet Dog Trainers
www.apdt.com

Karen Pryor Clicker Training
www.clickertraining.com

American Kennel Club Canine
Good Citizen
www.akc.org/events/cgc/index.cfm

American Brace Beagling
Association
*www.americanbracebeagling
association.com*

AKC Tracking
*www.akc.org/pdfs/events/tracking/
beginners_guide.pdf*

AKC Rally
*www.akc.org/events/rally/getting_
started.cfm*

AKC Agility
www.akc.org/events/agility/index.cfm

AKC Beagle Field Trials
*www.akc.org/events/field_trials/beagles/
getting_started.cfm*

UKC Beagle Program
www.ukcdogs.com

AKC Junior Showmanship Program
www.akc.org/kids_juniors/index.cfm

National 4-H Program
www.4-h.org

Therapy Dogs International, Inc.
www.tdi-dog.org

Delta Society
www.deltasociety.org

Pet Loss and Grief Support

Association for Pet Loss and
    Bereavement
www.aplb.org

Pet Loss Support Page
www.pet-loss.net

Pet Loss Grief Support
www.petloss.com

Rainbows Bridge
www.rainbowsbridge.com

Travel Resources

Pets Welcome
www.petswelcome.com

Official Pet Hotels
www.officialpethotels.com

Dog Friendly
www.dogfriendly.com

Travel Pets
www.travelpets.com

Pet Sitters International
www.petsit.com.

National Association of Professional
    Pet Sitters
www.petsitters.org

Index

THE TEAM BEHIND THE *TRAIN YOUR DOG* DVD

Host **Nicole Wilde** is a certified Pet Dog Trainer and internationally recognized author and lecturer. Her books include *So You Want to be a Dog Trainer* and *Help for Your Fearful Dog* (Phantom Publishing). In addition to working with dogs, Nicole has been working with wolves and wolf hybrids for over fifteen years and is considered an expert in the field.

Host **Laura Bourhenne** is a Professional Member of the Association of Pet Dog Trainers, and holds a degree in Exotic Animal Training. She has trained many species of animals including several species of primates, birds of prey, and many more. Laura is striving to enrich the lives of pets by training and educating the people they live with.

Director **Leo Zahn** is an award winning director/cinematographer/editor of television commercials, movies, and documentaries. He has directed and edited more than a dozen instructional DVDs through the Picture Company, a subsidiary of Picture Palace, Inc., based in Los Angeles.